PROPERTY SERIES

Investing in Property for your Children

Catherine Dawson

Investing in Property for your Children
by Catherine Dawson

© 2008 Lawpack Publishing

Lawpack Publishing Limited
76–89 Alscot Road
London SE1 3AW

www.lawpack.co.uk

Printed in Great Britain by Athenaeum Press Ltd, Gateshead, Tyne & Wear

ISBN: 978-1-905261-78-9

Exclusion of Liability and Disclaimer

Contents

About the author

Catherine Dawson is a trained and experienced reseacher with an MA in Social Research. Her speciality is housing issues and she is the author of several books on property, including *The Complete Guide to Buying Repossessed Property Bargains* also published by Lawpack. Since 1996 she has been a shareholder of a growing and successful family property development company for which she conducts all the research and development work, including how to make sure the children are left the best possible inheritance.

Important facts

This book is for use in England and Wales and Scotland. It is not intended for use in Northern Ireland.

The information it contains has been carefully compiled from professional sources, but its accuracy is not guaranteed, as laws and regulations may change or be subject to differing interpretations. The law is stated as at 1 July 2008.

Neither this nor any other publication can take the place of a solicitor or accountant on important legal matters. As with any legal or financial matter, common sense should determine whether you need the assistance of a solicitor or accountant rather than rely solely on the information and forms in this book.

Introduction

This book is a complete guide to investing in property for your children. It covers the different types of property investment available to parents and includes all the related information about leaving property in Wills, setting up trusts, paying Inheritance Tax and protecting your investment. It is aimed at anyone who is thinking about investing in property as a means of saving and making money for their child's future.

I am a shareholder of Dawson Properties Ltd, a family-run business for which I conduct the research and development. My brothers and sister are involved in the company and we all work hard so that we can leave a good inheritance for our children, nephews and nieces. We have done this by setting up a property business through which we buy houses cheaply, renovate and refurbish them, and then let to students and working people. The money from the rental income is used to renovate and refurbish existing properties and to buy more properties. It is our intention to pass this property business on to our children when they are adults. They can then decide whether they want to keep the business running or whether they wish to sell the properties, spend the money or invest elsewhere.

We are following in the footsteps of our grandfather who also owned properties that he left in trust for us. My grandfather's trust worked very well – it was well managed and generated a significant rental income from the properties. The trust reinvested the rental income until each of us reached the age of 18, from which time it was paid direct to us. We became legal owners of the properties when each of us reached the age of 32. My grandfather had decided that this would be a good age for us to become the owners as we would be settled into our working and family lives and would not squander the money. Although we haven't yet set up a trust for our children, we are considering a similar type of scheme that we can set up in the future.

Since we set up our business the property market has performed well, with the property company providing interesting and varied employment, in addition to building a good nest egg for the next generation of the family. In this book I hope to pass on this information to other parents who are interested in investing in property for their children.

There are a variety of ways that, as a parent, you can invest in property for your children. Perhaps you have decided that investing in property is a useful way to save money for your child's education; or maybe you feel that property prices have risen so much that you would like to buy a house in which your children can live, either now or when they leave home in the future. Although property prices are now falling, many first-time buyers are still priced out of the market, and this will continue to be the case unless property prices fall drastically. Many parents feel that they would like the security of knowing that their child has somewhere to live, despite these fluctuations in the housing market. Other parents want to invest in property to leave to their children when they die, perhaps, like my grandfather, setting up a trust so that their children's inheritance is well managed and maintained according to their wishes. This book offers advice about all these types of property investment, providing a detailed summary of the options available to you as parents.

Once you have read this book you will be able to:

- understand the best way to invest in property for your child;

- understand tax issues and know how to reduce tax liability;

- know the most efficient way to raise capital for your property investment;

- know how to choose the best property;

- know how to manage and maintain your investment property;

- understand how to protect your child's inheritance; and

- know the best way to leave your property to your child.

Part 1 offers advice about planning your investment. The first chapter helps you to decide whether property investment is the most appropriate type of investment for you and your family, offering advice about monitoring the housing market and knowing when is the right time to invest. Chapter 2 discusses issues surrounding inheritance legislation, rules and regulations. In chapters 3 and 4, information is offered about Inheritance Tax and exemptions, with other types of property tax discussed in chapter 5. The final chapter in this section helps you plan your finances so that you can decide whether this type of investment is the most appropriate for your financial circumstances.

Part 2 discusses the different types of property investment, including helping your child onto the property ladder, buying a property for your student child and investing in a second home.

The final part of the book offers advice about protecting your investment. Chapter 10 considers ways in which you can protect against financial loss, such as arranging appropriate insurance and managing and maintaining your investment property. Chapters 11 and 12 consider ways to protect your child's inheritance and reduce your tax liability by making an appropriate Will and/or setting up a trust.

As circumstances, wants and needs vary between families, a number of different scenarios are provided at the end of the book, guiding parents through the different options that are available. Checklists for investing in, choosing and viewing appropriate properties are provided in Appendices 1–4 and alternative investment opportunities for your children are discussed in Appendix 5. Sample forms are available in Appendix 6. Finally, useful addresses, websites and further reading are provided for parents who wish to follow up or act upon any of the information provided in this book. I hope that you find this book interesting and useful and I wish you every success with your property investment.

Part 1: Planning your investment

CHAPTER 1

Choosing to invest in property

Property investment has become popular over the last few decades as you can make substantial profits, even in times of financial uncertainty, as long as your investment is well researched and carefully planned. If you are interested in buying property as an investment for your children, there are a variety of methods that you can choose, depending on your personal circumstances, experiences and the finances you have available.

To invest successfully in property you need to monitor market trends and prospects and have a clear understanding of the difference between long- and short-term trends and how this will affect your investment. You also need to make sure that you have the necessary skills, experience and motivation to undertake this type of investment, and you need to conduct detailed and systematic research.

Knowing about the types of property investment

There are several ways in which parents can help provide for their children through property investment and the method that you choose will depend on the following factors:

* your financial circumstances;

* your skills, knowledge and experience;

* your present property ownership;

* your family circumstances, wants and needs;

* the type of investment you want;

* the state of the economy;

* the performance of the housing market;

* the age of your children.

The different types of property investment are discussed below.

Helping your children onto the property ladder

If your children are struggling to buy their first house, you can help them onto the property ladder by providing financial help, acting as a guarantor or taking out a joint or family offset mortgage (see later) to help them purchase their house. If you decide to follow this route, not only are you investing in property, but you are also making sure that your child has somewhere to live. However, with this type of arrangement you must make sure that you and your child are protected, legally and financially (see chapter 7).

Buying property for your student child

If your child is about to go away to college or university, you may be thinking about buying a home for him to live in while he studies. This could also be a good investment opportunity, depending on the location of the property, the price and whether you decide to let other rooms to fellow students. It will give you peace of mind to know that your child has somewhere safe and secure to live and that he will not have problems with rent or be at the mercy of unscrupulous landlords. However, you need to have a thorough understanding of the rules and regulations involved in letting student accommodation and be aware of the problems that can arise. For example, would it affect your relationship with your child if you had to take his friends to court for rent arrears or damage to your property?

Investing in a second property for your child

Other parents may decide to buy a second property in their own name as an investment for their child. This could be to sell once your child reaches a significant age, or a property in which your child can live when he decides to leave home. Again, this can be a good investment if you choose the property wisely, but you need to make sure that you understand all the issues surrounding property inheritance and gifts. You also need to undertake careful and systematic research so that you do not lose out financially on your investment. Buying a second property is discussed in chapter 9. Advice and information about finding and choosing a suitable investment property is offered in the Appendices. Issues surrounding property inheritance are covered in the following chapter.

Leaving property to your child when you die

Many parents invest in property for their children by leaving their home to them when they die. If you are already a property owner and you are intending to leave your home to your children, you need to think about maximising their inheritance while minimising their tax liability. This should be the case with any property that you are intending to leave to your children and these issues are discussed in chapters 2, 3, 4 and 5.

Also, you should note that children under the age of 18 cannot own land or buildings so, if you have children under that age, you need to consider whether it might be appropriate to set up a trust that will manage and maintain your property if you and your spouse die before your children reach 18. There are various types of trust that could be used for this purpose, and tax savings can be made if you choose this type of investment. More information about trusts is provided in chapter 12 and the different ways in which trusts can be used are presented in a number of scenarios at the end of this book.

Assessing the advantages and disadvantages

Before you invest in property you need to undertake a careful assessment of the advantages and disadvantages of the type of investment, so that you can decide whether it is the most appropriate way to invest for your family. These are listed in Table 1.

TABLE 1: THE ADVANTAGES AND DISADVANTAGES OF PROPERTY INVESTMENT

ADVANTAGES	DISADVANTAGES
There is potential to make a substantial profit when you decide to sell.	There is potential to make a substantial loss when you decide to sell. Although the property market has performed very well in the last 15 years, especially when compared with other types of investment, we are now experiencing a fall in prices and some experts are predicting a market crash in the next few years. This could have serious financial implications for property investors who have overstretched themselves financially.
Fluctuations in the market can work to your advantage, if you choose to sell at the right time.	Fluctuations in the market can work to your disadvantage, if you have to sell at the wrong time, or if you decide to sell when your child reaches a significant age. Unforeseeable changes in your financial circumstances may force you to sell and lose out financially. It is important to protect yourself and your family with a financial contingency fund (see chapter 6)

	and adequate insurance (see chapter 10). If possible, you should try to be flexible about the date that you intend to sell so that you are not at the mercy of short-term fluctuations (see below).
Your cash is tied up in an investment and therefore cannot be spent recklessly.	You may not be able to afford to tie up large sums of money, and may lose out financially if you have to sell quickly to raise cash. This problem can be avoided by spreading your investment and taking advantage of low risk investment opportunities (see below).
There are substantial profits to be made through letting property. Interestingly, despite recent drops in house prices, rental yields are still high in some parts of the UK. This is because the rental market is buoyant – first-time buyers are still priced out of the market and have to rent; separation and divorce increases the number of single people who cannot afford to buy; students and migrant workers are always looking for accommodation to rent and many potential buyers are waiting for the housing market to settle before they buy. However, the rental market is saturated in some parts of the UK, so you must make sure that	You may be unable to find tenants for your property and can find it difficult to meet mortgage repayments. Your property could be repossessed. Some tenants can cause all sorts of problems and initiating court proceedings can be time-consuming and stressful. Some of these problems can be avoided by arranging suitable insurance (see chapter 10). Letting property creates restrictions on what you can and can't do in your property, such as fitting fire doors, using fire resistant furniture and arranging gas and electricity servicing and inspections (see chapter 8).

tenants are available in the area and are willing to live in the type of property that you intend to let (see chapter 8).

Careful investment and development will enhance the value of the property.	Properties can be expensive and time-consuming to maintain. Inappropriate or poor development can reduce the value of your property. Choosing and working with contractors and traders can be difficult and stressful for those without previous experience.
It is still possible to obtain a buy-to-let mortgage at a competitive rate. However, due to the 'credit crunch' you will have to convince the lender that the property is suitable for the rental market and that there are tenants available who will be able to pay the rent you require. Some lenders will not provide buy-to-let mortgages for certain types of property, such as some city centre apartments. You will also need to demonstrate that you have the required knowledge and expertise to make the venture work and be able to put down at least 10 per cent deposit.	Taking out a mortgage on a second property may influence your chances of getting a mortgage if you decide to move at a later date. You may be unable to meet mortgage repayments if you are sick or lose your job. There may be age restrictions attached to your preferred mortgage or, depending on the type of mortgage that you choose, you may have to pay higher rates on life cover because of your age.
You are free to use the property as you wish,	Restrictive covenants, type of ownership and the area in which the property is

subject to planning regulations and relevant legislation.	located may restrict what you are able to do with the property. Listed building status could seriously restrict what you can do with a property.
Tax incentives, discount schemes and grants are available. Setting up a trust or buying property in your child's name can reduce the tax bill for your child.	Your tax liability, or that of your children, could be considerable without careful tax planning (see chapter 5). Property tax is complex and you will need to seek professional advice if in doubt.
Interest rates could work in your favour. This could be by an interest rate drop or because you take out the right mortgage for the market conditions.	Interest rates could rise and increase your monthly outgoings considerably, or you could choose the wrong type of mortgage for the market conditions.

Depending on the type of investment that you wish to undertake, there are other advantages and disadvantages that you should be aware of. These are discussed in chapters 7, 8 and 9.

Analysing housing market trends

To invest successfully in property you need to have a thorough understanding of current and future economic and market conditions, and understand how they relate to the housing market. When the economy expands, lenders tend to extend too much credit and consumers are happy to accept this credit because they have confidence in the housing market. However, this means that there is a much greater risk of loss and default when conditions are less favourable.

Excessive borrowing has led to financial crises in the past and it is feared that many homeowners who have overstretched their borrowing will suffer if interest rates rise, or when favourable fixed-rate mortgage deals come to an end. Recent figures indicate that the number of repossessions in the UK rose to 27,100 in 2007, up from 22,400 in 2006 according to the Council of Mortgage Lenders (CML), and experts fear that this figure will rise to over 45,000 in 2008.

Assessing the risk

You need to undertake a careful assessment of your present and future finances when you analyse housing market trends. It is important to consider these in terms of the amount you can afford to borrow, the interest rates you will have to pay and how these may rise or fall in the future. If the housing market begins to slow down, how will this affect your financial investment, over both the short and the long term? You must make sure that you do not put your family and your home at risk through unwise investment choices. More information about all these issues is provided in chapter 6.

Monitoring the market

It is important to monitor the housing market and economy so that you can understand what is happening on both a national and local level. This will help you to assess whether property investment for your child is the most appropriate and sensible investment given the present conditions and future trends. It will also help you to decide if and when to sell if you are already a property owner.

Knowing where to find information

The British Bankers' Association (BBA) represents the banking industry in the UK. From this organisation you can receive useful information about rates of mortgage lending and credit card borrowing, which provides an indication of how the housing market and economy are performing on a monthly basis (www.bba.org.uk).

Another useful source for monitoring the housing market is the Land Registry (www.landregistry.gov.uk). This organisation produces the Land Registry House Price Index, which uses sales data collected on all residential transactions, whether for cash or with a mortgage, in England and Wales since April 2000. It is possible to search the Index at a national, regional, county or London borough level. The survey contains details of over seven million sales and claims to be the only complete record of residential property transactions in England and Wales. If you live in

Scotland, a similar survey is produced by the Registers of Scotland Executive Agency (www.ros.gov.uk).

The Council of Mortgage Lenders (CML) is the trade association for the mortgage lending industry in the UK. It produces regular research articles and in-depth reports on the performance of the housing market. A variety of publications can be downloaded from its website and are useful for keeping abreast of what is happening in the housing market and for providing advice and information about property investment (www.cml.org.uk).

The Halifax produces the Halifax House Price Index, which is based on their mortgage lending in the UK and provides a useful indication of house prices and property market trends. On the website (www.hbosplc.com) you can access a regional house price map, a house price calculator and quarterly regional comments on the movement of the housing market. A similar survey is produced by the Nationwide, based on their lending data for properties at the post-survey approval stage (www.nationwide.co.uk).

Predicting investment trends and prospects

If you are hoping to make a good return on your investment for your children, you need property prices to continue to rise over the term of your investment. Yet how do you know that this will happen? How is it possible to predict the price of property in ten or 20 years' time? How do you know that your property will realise the best possible price when your child is due to receive the proceeds from the sale if sold during your lifetime or when he inherits the property after your death? Although certain aspects of this type of investment are beyond your control, such as the date at which you are going to die, there are other predictions that can be made, based on careful research and judgement.

Assessing past performance

To gain a better understanding of the trends and prospects of the housing market it is useful to look at how the market has performed in the past.

The Nationwide house price survey began in 1973 and since that time house prices have increased by an average of 9 per cent a year. This compares to an average rate of inflation of 7 per cent a year over the same period. The Halifax House Price Index was first produced in 1983 and over that time the Index shows that house prices have increased by 8 per cent a year, while inflation has increased by 4.5 per cent a year.

It is important to note that these prices are average figures and that some regions in the UK perform better than others. Despite this, it is easy to see that house prices have beaten inflation over the last 25 to 35 years, and therefore, buying property has represented a good long-term investment. However, as a short-term investment the situation can be very different, with house prices fluctuating significantly. For example, in the five years from 1990 to 1995 house prices fell by around 10 per cent, yet in the 13 years since 1995 house prices have more than trebled in many parts of the UK.

At time of writing house prices are beginning to fall again and opinion is divided about whether we will experience another property market crash. Some experts are looking across the Atlantic to the problems experienced by the 'credit crunch' in the USA, predicting that similar problems could occur in the UK, and that the housing market will be seriously affected if this happens.

However, this should not deter would-be investors as history indicates that this will be a short-term problem. Indeed, this could mean that property prices fall considerably and that there are good bargains available for those who wish to invest in property. Over the long term, if previous trends continue, your property should continue to rise in value.

Assessing short- and long-term trends

Short- and long-term trends need to be taken into account when you consider your investment strategy. For example, if you are buying a property for your minor child (i.e. under 18) that you then wish to sell when he reaches 18, perhaps to pay for his university education, you may be at the mercy of short-term fluctuations. This is because you have set a rigid 'sell-by' date (i.e. the age at which he reaches 18). Although the price of the property may have risen over the long term, if the property market has slumped when your child reaches 18, you could lose the gains that you have made. In this case you may be better holding onto the property for a little longer until property prices have risen again before you decide to sell. If you choose to do this, you would need to make sure that you had access to other funds to pay for his university education in the short term until you could release the funds in your investment property by selling.

It is also important to consider the trends and prospects of other types of investment. This will help you decide whether your money might be better invested elsewhere and enable you to spread your investment risk. For example, it is important to have money available for your children's education if the housing market is not performing well when they start college or university and you therefore decide that it is not a good time to invest in a property for them. Other assets, such as shares, can produce better returns than the property market, but this type of investment is much more volatile. In general, bonds and high interest savings accounts will not provide as good a return as property has done over the last 35 years, but they are safe options because you will not lose the original money you have invested (see Appendix 5).

Obtaining financial advice

If you feel that you do not have the necessary knowledge and skills to make suitable investment decisions, you should seek advice from a financial adviser. When choosing a financial adviser you should note that only firms and their agents authorised by the Financial Services Authority (FSA) are allowed to give financial advice. The FSA is an independent, non-governmental body, accountable to Treasury Ministers and through them to Parliament. The FSA is operationally independent of the government, although the FSA Board that sets the overall policy is appointed by the Treasury. It is funded entirely by the firms that it regulates, setting the standards that must be met and taking action against firms that fail to meet the required standards. If the financial adviser that you use is regulated by the FSA, you may be entitled to compensation if he goes out of business. More information about the FSA and the standards required of financial advisers can be obtained from their website (www.fsa.gov.uk).

While the FSA regulates the financial services industry, the Personal Finance Society (PFS) is the professional body for financial advisers and people in related roles (www.thepfs.org). The PFS is a member of the Chartered Insurance Institute and has adopted their Code of Ethics and Conduct, which encourages the highest professional and ethical standards in insurance and financial services. You can find a financial adviser in your area by using the online directory. Alternatively, visit the Institute of Financial Planning website to search for a qualified financial planner (www.financialplanning.org.uk).

The terms 'financial planner' and 'financial adviser' tend to be used interchangeably – both should be able to offer advice about your finances and both should be able to help you to plan for the future. You should check that the person you choose has at least the basic level qualifications of a Certificate in Financial Planning (or its predecessor the Financial Planning Certificate/FPC) or the Certificate for Financial Advisers (CeFA), which gives the adviser authorisation to give advice to clients.

When choosing a financial adviser don't be tempted to use those who cold call. If you are suspicious about a person or organisation, consult the FSA website above to access its list of unauthorised firms that are currently targeting UK investors or for more information about fraudulent activity such as scams and swindles.

Beating inflation

The Consumer Prices Index (CPI) is used to measure inflation in the UK. Using this method, changes in the prices of selected household goods are used to determine the rate of inflation. Currently, the UK inflation rate is above average for the European Union as a whole, so you need to make sure that any investment that you make for your child's future is not at the mercy of inflation and any future rises that may occur. Inflation determines the real return on your investment. It can have a major impact on the value of your money and can affect what your child is able to buy in the future, if he chooses to sell the property that you have bought as an investment for him. For more information about the CPI and for up-to-date figures, visit www.statistics.gov.uk.

When economic growth is strong more money chases fewer goods and services, which pushes up prices and leads to higher inflation. When this occurs, interest rates are used to keep growth broadly in line with its long-run trend of around 2.5 per cent each year. Higher interest rates tend to discourage borrowing and encourage saving, which should slow the economy. Lower rates encourage borrowing and have the opposite effect. Movements in interest rates affect the overall level of demand in the economy and so can have a powerful influence on the inflation rate. Therefore, it is important to monitor inflation and interest rates carefully to make the most of your investment.

Although higher inflation rates tend to be good for borrowers and bad for investors, you need to consider this link between inflation and interest rates when making your investment. If you intend to take out a mortgage on a property, the real value of your mortgage could be reduced considerably in times of high inflation, so this could work in your favour, but only if interest rates are favourable. Therefore, if you have cash to invest it may not be prudent to invest all your money by buying outright when inflation is high. Instead, you could decide to borrow on the property, or you could look to other types of investment for your child. More information about alternative types of investment for your child is offered in Appendix 5.

Investing in equities

Investing in equities is a possible way to beat inflation if you have money to invest and as long as inflation is not severe. You can choose low, medium or high risk equities and can choose the type of fund in which you wish to invest. Ethical funds are available and, at present, they are not any riskier than other types of funds. Indeed, recent research by Deutsche Bank found that when the FTSE 350 companies are ranked according to ethical criteria, the top 10 per cent outperform the bottom 10 per cent in financial returns by more than 7.5 per cent per year. This illustrates that you do not have to compromise financial returns for ethical principles. To find a financial adviser that specialises in ethical funds, visit the Ethical Investors Association (EIA) at www.ethicalinvestment.org.uk.

Real Estate Investment Trusts

If you are interested in property investment, it is possible to invest your money in a Real Estate Investment Trust (REIT), which includes commercial property, offices, shops, factories and warehouses, but you will need to choose a specialist fund manager that offers this service. Buying shares in a REIT would allow you to invest in various types of property without the problems associated with physically buying into bricks and mortar. However, if all your money is tied up in property you would be particularly at risk from any serious downturn in the property market. More information about REITs can be obtained from the London Stock Exchange website (www.londonstockexchange.com).

Assessing skills, knowledge and experience

If you feel that the market conditions, trends and prospects are right for property investment, you need to assess your skills, knowledge and experience. Again, this will help you ascertain whether this is the most appropriate type of investment for you. The following questions will help you do this:

1   Why have you decided to invest in property for your child?

2   Have you considered the other types of investment opportunity that are available to you, as a parent?

3   Do you understand the advantages and disadvantages inherent in property investment?

4   What experiences and knowledge can you, personally, bring to the property investment?

5   What experiences and knowledge can other members of the family bring to your property investment?

6   Do you have a thorough understanding of the financial implications for your child, especially in terms of tax liability? Do you understand the rules and regulations?

7   Do you understand how trusts work and how you could make tax savings for your child by putting your property in an appropriate trust?

8   Do you know enough about investing in property to make a sound decision? If not, how do you intend to increase your knowledge and avoid mistakes?

9 Do you have the required skills? If not, what are you going to do to acquire the appropriate skills?

10 Are you able to negotiate and bargain with others to receive the best deal?

11 Are you able to delegate?

12 Do you have good project management skills?

13 Are you confident and experienced enough to deal with contractors, tradespeople and service providers?

14 Do you understand the rules and regulations about rental property?

15 Do you have good financial management skills?

16 What contingency plans and funds do you have in place, should your investment fail?

17 Are you putting your home and family at risk in any way, especially financially and emotionally?

18 Do you know how to protect your investment? Have you looked into the various types of insurance that will be required? Do you understand how to monitor the market to protect your investment?

Author's note

Our family is very lucky in terms of skills and knowledge when it comes to property investment. I have one brother who is a chartered accountant and another who is a financial manager for an international company. My third brother is self-taught in all aspects of property development and improvement and also has a Masters in Business Administration (MBA). I am trained in research methods, specialising in the private rental sector. My sister has many years' experience as an administrator and is a very competent painter and decorator. My sister-in-law trained in management and accountancy and my partner is an IT consultant and web designer. Together we have most of the skills required to run a successful property business. However, that is not to say that we get complacent or take profits for granted. We all understand that the property market can be very unpredictable and that it is important for us to monitor the market and update our skills and knowledge on a regular basis.

Conducting background research

Thorough background research is essential to the success of your investment, whatever type you choose. When conducting your research you must be aware of the source of your information so that you can make sure that it is valid and reliable. This is of particular importance when obtaining information from the Internet. Anyone can post information on the Internet and you need to think about their motives for doing so. Why do they want their information to enter the public domain? Do they have a vested interest? Are they trying to sell something?

When surfing the Net, always check the 'about us' section so that you can find out more about the organisation or individual of the site you are looking at. Find out the country of origin, if possible, as information, advice and products may differ between countries, especially concerning tax and legal issues. The FSA believes that all websites offering investment and financial products should provide a straightforward and balanced overall impression of the product and a clear indication of the risks and drawbacks. If the site you are visiting does not do this, you should look elsewhere. Try to cross-reference the information you have found, using a different source, such as a recognised trade or professional association, or a consumer group such as Which?. Never give personal details to organisations that you are unsure of and don't hand over money or bank details until you are completely sure that the organisation you have chosen is reputable.

Sources of information

When conducting background research, there are two main sources of information – primary sources and secondary sources. Obtaining information from primary sources involves first-hand observation and investigation, whereas secondary sources are studies that other people have made of a subject, such as research studies or journal articles. Through using as many sources as possible you will be able to gather more valid and reliable information. The different sources of information for property investment are listed in Table 2.

TABLE 2: SOURCES OF PROPERTY INFORMATION

PRIMARY SOURCES	SECONDARY SOURCES
You, your family, friends and colleagues	National Statistics
Estate agents/letting agents	Which? reports
Vendors	Mortgage company reports
Landlords	Building society analyses
Property developers	Building Federation reports
Land registers	Academic journals and reports
Mortgage lenders	Government analyses and reports
Census data	Economic and market reviews
Surveyors	Housing and property books
Conveyancers	Housing charity research
Solicitors	Trade association research
Tradespeople and service providers	Social trends analyses
Builders	Property newspapers and magazines
Tenants	Financial newspapers and magazines
Neighbours	Local newspapers
Citizens Advice Bureaux staff	Local radio
Council staff	Local and national television
Planning applications	Professional association reports
Town/city development plans	Property/housing websites

In addition to conducting thorough background research, all successful property investors conduct comprehensive location, neighbourhood and individual property research. Checklists for undertaking this type of research are offered in Appendices 2 and 3.

Summary

Property investment has become popular as parents can make large profits on careful investment. However, it is important to consider the advantages and disadvantages of investing in property, undertake a thorough analysis of market conditions, consider personal strengths and weaknesses and conduct detailed background research before making your investment decisions. Although it is impossible to know how the housing market will perform over the next few decades, it is possible to make careful and reasoned judgements based on what has happened in the past. Also, you need to view your investment as a long-term strategy and be flexible so that you are not at the mercy of short-term fluctuations in the market. This should help to protect your investment and ensure that you maximise the funds that are available for your child in the future. You should also consider seeking independent financial advice if you feel that you do not have the required level of knowledge and understanding to make your own decisions.

If you have decided that you are interested in investing in property, and that your strategy can be flexible and not at the mercy of short-term fluctuations, you need to gain a thorough understanding of the issues involved when property is passed from you to your child.

CHAPTER 2

Knowing about property inheritance

There are many issues, rules and regulations associated with property inheritance and if you are hoping to leave property to your children when you die, it is important that you understand these. This will help you to make the right property investment decisions and enable you to maximise your child's inheritance while minimising his tax liability on your death.

This chapter offers advice and information about inheriting property, transferring property after death, choosing what to do with an inherited property, the Inheritance Act and the implications of your investment decisions on your children.

Inheriting property

The way in which your children can inherit property depends on the type of ownership, the age of your children, whether you have written a Will and whether you have set up a trust. You should note that it is not possible for a child under the age of 18 to legally own land or buildings. Therefore, if you have bought an investment property, or you intend to leave your own home to your children, you should provide specific arrangements in your Will. If you do not write a Will, your property will be distributed according to the laws of intestacy, which may go against your wishes (see below). If your children are under 18 and they inherit property, their share is looked after by your personal representatives acting as trustees until your children reach the age of 18. A personal representative is a person who administers a deceased person's estate. If there is a Will and the personal representative is named in it, he is known as an executor. If there is no Will, or he has been appointed by the court, he is known as an administrator. Information about writing a suitable Will is provided in chapter 11.

You can set up a trust to manage and maintain your property if you should die before your child reaches 18. Trusts can be set up during your lifetime or on your death and provide a useful way to manage, maintain and control your property until your child is old enough to inherit. Information about setting up a trust and the different trusts that may be suitable for your needs is provided in chapter 12.

The type of ownership of your property also has implications for whether you can leave your share of the property to your children. This includes ownership based on a 'joint tenancy' and a 'tenancy in common'.

Joint tenancy

A joint tenancy is a way for two or more people to own a property. Cohabiting couples often have this type of agreement, but it is also possible for a parent and child (or children) to decide upon this type of ownership, which can be held by up to four people (see chapter 7). When one owner dies the other owners of the property automatically receive the deceased owner's share. This means that there is no need for a Will to be drawn up to pass on the property and that joint owners cannot leave their share to other people in their Will.

An advantage to this type of ownership is that property is transferred to the surviving joint owners without the delay and cost of probate (see below). A disadvantage is that if an owner wishes to leave his share in the property to someone else, other than the other joint owners, he must first sever his joint tenancy. You can do this by serving a 'notice of severance' on the other owner. This can be drafted by your solicitor for a small fee or you can draft a notice of severance yourself. This must be in writing and all that is necessary is to write that 'I [name] give notice to [names of other co-owners] of my intention to sever the joint tenancy of [address]. Dated [date]', and sign it. You should send this notice by recorded or registered post to the other owner(s) as proof that it has been sent.

Once this notice has been served, there is nothing that the other owner can do to prevent the severance. This is useful if you have split from your partner or spouse and you wish to leave your share in the property to your children, rather than to your ex-partner. If the property is registered with the Land Registry, you will need to inform it that the severance has occurred. You can do this by completing form RX1, which is available from the Land Registry (www.landregistry.gov.uk). You should note, also, that with this type of ownership, if you are in debt when you die, in certain circumstances a court can order that the inherited share of your property is used to pay your creditors, if the creditors have applied for an insolvency administration order. This could have a significant negative impact on your child's inheritance.

More information about joint tenancies can be obtained from your local Citizens Advice Bureau (CAB) or from the Community Legal Service (CLS) website (www.clsdirect.org.uk).

Tenancy in common

In this type of agreement each joint owner owns a separate share in the property. On the death of one of the joint owners, his share passes to whoever has been named in his Will or, if a Will has not been drawn up, it is transferred through the laws of intestacy (see below). Unlike a joint tenancy, the share of the deceased owner does not pass automatically to the other owners, so it is very important to draw up a Will to make sure that your share of the property goes to the person (or people) you want it to. If you are divorced or separated and there are children from other marriages whom you do not wish to inherit your share of the property, it is imperative that you write a Will in which you make this clear. More information about writing a Will in cases of separation and divorce is provided in chapter 11.

More information about tenancies in common can be obtained from your local CAB or from the CLS website (www.clsdirect.org.uk). Information about drawing up a Will is provided in chapter 11.

The laws of intestacy

If a person has not made a Will when he dies, he is said to have died 'intestate'. In these circumstances there are certain laws that set out who should deal with the intestate's affairs and who should inherit his estate, including property. The rules of intestacy state that the closest relative of the deceased should deal with the estate, and this is laid out in a specific order.

If there are several people with an equal right to deal with the estate, 'letters of administration' (the legal document which authorises the administrator to deal with the deceased's estate – see below) are normally given to the first three applicants. In cases where there is a dispute, an application is made to the Probate Court to decide who will take responsibility. This process can be costly, time-consuming and damaging to family relationships, so it is important to avoid these problems by making a Will (see chapter 11). For example, your children, if they are over the age of 18, are second in line to deal with your estate after your spouse or civil partner. Would this cause problems in cases where your children disagreed with the way your affairs were being administered by your spouse, especially if you have remarried? Would you trust your spouse to follow your wishes, or indeed understand what you would want to do with your property, if you had not listed these in a Will?

If you die without making a Will, the Administration of Estates Act 1925 sets out who gets what from your estate. The rules are complex and depend on your personal situation. However, as far as your children are concerned the following rules are the most important to note:

If you leave a spouse and children, your spouse receives:

- 'personal chattels' (These are defined in law and are taken to mean personal items such as cars, jewellery and other household goods. It does not include houses, bank accounts, investments or businesses, which instead are added to the deceased's estate to be distributed as described below.);

- the first £125,000 of the deceased's estate (If the estate is less than £125,000, the deceased's surviving spouse or civil partner will receive the whole of the estate.);

- a 'life interest' in half of what is left. 'Life interest' means the income or interest of any money that is invested, but not the money itself. The capital (the original amount) passes to your children when the surviving husband or wife dies. Your children share between them half of what is left, if they are over 18 years old, and the other half of what is left when their surviving parent dies. Illegitimate and adopted children are included in this, but stepchildren get nothing, unless they are named in a Will. Therefore, if you have remarried and your spouse is not your child's parent, you must make a Will so that your child can inherit his share of your estate.

If you leave children and no spouse:

- your children share everything equally.

Probate

Probate is the legal process used to prove that a Will is valid, to appoint executors and settle the estate of the deceased. When someone has died a 'grant of representation' is issued by the courts. This is a document that enables the person named in it to deal with the assets and belongings of the deceased and allows for money to be collected, property to be sold or transferred and debts to be paid. In England, Wales and Northern Ireland the two most common types of grant of representation are:

1 **A grant of probate.** This is where the deceased has left a Will. The executor, who has usually been named in the Will, applies for a grant of probate from the probate registry. This is a legal document that enables the executor to deal with the deceased person's assets, which includes property.

2 **A grant of letters of administration.** This is where the deceased has not left a Will. In this case a close relative applies to the probate registry to administer the assets of the deceased. If permission is granted he obtains the legal document and becomes an 'administrator' of the estate.

More information about probate registries can be obtained from Her Majesty's Courts Service (www.hmcourts-service.gov.uk). If you live in

Scotland, relatives apply for a 'grant of confirmation'. More information about this procedure can be obtained from the HM Revenue & Customs website (www.hmrc.gov.uk) or from the Scottish Courts website (www.scotcourts.gov.uk).

Understanding the procedure for transferring property after your death

The procedure for transferring property after your death varies depending on whether the land is registered or not. The procedure is more complicated if the land is unregistered, so you can make the process easier for your executors or administrators by making sure that your land is registered before you die. (If your land is unregistered when you die, your children's administrators or executors will need to employ the services of a solicitor to prepare the necessary transfer documents, which can be costly and time-consuming.) It is also important to register the land because it proves that you own your land and protects you (or your children when the property is passed to them) against claims on your land if someone were to try to encroach on it.

Visit the Land Registry website (www.landregistry.gov.uk) where, for a small charge, you will be able to find out whether your property is registered by entering the address details or the title number of the property. In general, all properties bought or remortgaged since 1 April 1998 will be registered and most properties bought after 1 December 1990 will be registered.

Currently, the Land Registry believes that just over 60 per cent of properties are registered and it is now compulsory that land is registered when it is sold. If you find that your property is not registered, you should visit the Land Registry website; contact the register development helpline (0800 432 0432) or send an email to registerland@landregistry.gsi.gov.uk for advice about registering your land.

Once your land is registered the executor or administrator who has been appointed to deal with your estate will have to send the following to the Land Registry:

- a form which transfers ownership, called an 'assent' or 'appropriation'. If the property is leasehold, the landlord must be notified of the change of ownership and is entitled to receive a copy of the form. Your children will not have to pay Stamp Duty Land Tax (SDLT) when the property is transferred in this way (see chapter 5);

- the original or official copy of the grant of probate or letters of administration;

- the appropriate fee, if any (a fee calculator is available on the Land Registry website).

Once the correct procedure has been followed and the property has been transferred to your children, they must decide what they wish to do with the property (see below). You will make this process easier for them if you discuss the issues once they are old enough to understand.

Choosing what to do with an inherited property

If your children are over the age of 18 when they inherit, they must decide what they are going to do with the property. If your children are under the age of 18 when they inherit, these decisions will be made by the executors or trustees who have been appointed to deal with your estate. Although your children's inheritance will be held in trust until your children reach the age of 18, you may find it preferable to set up a trust of your choosing while you are alive, so that you can decide how the trust will be managed, controlled and administered (see chapter 12).

If you have very specific ideas about what you would like your children to do with the property that they inherit, you should discuss these with them, if they are old enough, so that they understand what they need to do. If your children are too young, you need to leave clear instructions with your executors or trustees, if you decide to set up a trust. The property cannot be transferred into your children's names until they are 18, so the trustees or executors will need to take this into account when deciding what to do with the property.

When a property has been inherited, there are three main options available to your children – keep the property and live in it, keep the property to let to tenants, or sell the property.

Keeping an inherited property

In cases where the property is kept, your children, if they are over the age of 18, should transfer ownership at the Land Registry (described above). Once your children have done this, they can sell the property, obtain a second mortgage at a later date and prove ownership if they are required to do so. As we have seen above, this process will be much easier for your executors or administrators if your land is registered before you die.

If your adult children are already property owners and they inherit another property from you, they need to decide whether to nominate one of their properties with their Tax Office as their main residence. This is because when they sell a property that is not their main residence any profits are subject to CGT (see chapter 5). They can change the property that they nominate at a later date if they wish.

If you still have a mortgage on your property, your adult children could be responsible for taking on mortgage payments when they inherit. These may be difficult for your children to meet if they are students or in low paid employment, and if mortgage payments are missed there may be a danger that their property could be repossessed by the lender. However, you can protect against this by taking out insurance that pays your mortgage on death (see chapter 10) or by stipulating in your Will that outstanding mortgage debt should be met from your estate.

If you have taken out a life insurance policy, your children or the person dealing with your estate will need to write to the relevant company informing it of the date of death and enclosing an original death certificate. The payment should be made without delay, although in certain circumstances, for example, where a person has committed suicide shortly after taking out the policy, the company may not pay out. If the payment takes more than two months, the company must pay interest on the amount due. Again, you should file all the relevant documents with your Will so that your children or their personal representatives are able to claim on the policy as soon as possible. More information about life insurance and life assurance policies is provided in chapter 10.

You should note that if the inherited property is still mortgaged, Inheritance Tax (IHT) and Capital Gains Tax (CGT) are assessed on net gains, which means that the mortgage will be taken into account when the amount of tax is calculated. More information about IHT is provided in chapter 3 and more information about CGT is provided in chapter 5.

If your children are under the age of 18, your executors (or trustees if you have left the property in trust) must act according to the wishes that you set out in your Will. For example, you could choose to ask that the property is kept in trust until the last child reaches the age of 18 or 25, and that it is then sold with the proceeds being distributed equally between your children. Specific information about setting up a trust is provided in chapter 12 and a number of different scenarios about leaving property in trust are provided at the end of this book.

Letting the property

If your adult children decide not to move into the property but instead want to let it to tenants, it is treated as a business for tax purposes and they will need to keep accounts and fill in a self-assessment tax return each year (see chapter 5). Again, your adult children may find it useful if you discuss these implications with them so that they understand what they will have to do if they decide to let a property that they have inherited.

In certain cases your adult children could inherit a property that has someone living in it, such as a tenant or a relative. If the property is tenanted, or your children decide to let the property at a later date, they must understand their obligations as a landlord. More information about becoming a landlord is provided in chapter 8. If a relative is still living in the property, you should leave instructions in your Will about what you wish to happen to this person and your children must adhere to the terms of your Will. If you leave specific instructions in your Will, your children will be able to understand your wishes and will not need to employ the services of a solicitor to sort out problems that could arise.

If your children are under the age of 18, you need to provide specific instructions about how you wish your property to be managed on their behalf until they are old enough to legally own the property; for example, you could set up a trust through which you ask that the property is let to tenants with the proceeds from the rental income being invested in equities. The profits from this investment could then be distributed to your child when he reaches a significant age, with the property transferred into his name when he reaches the age of 18. If you choose this option you need to set up a trust and appoint trustees who are competent and happy to let the accommodation and who are able to invest the rental income in a way that will maximise returns. The trustees are responsible for making sure that all appropriate taxes are paid.

Selling an inherited property

If your adult children do not want to live in the inherited property or let it to tenants, they will need to think about selling the house. To do this they will need to produce a Home Information Pack (HIP) and make sure that they present their property in the best light to obtain the best selling price possible (see chapter 10). They will also need to find out whether there are any tax implications if they decide to sell (see chapter 5).

If your children are under the age of 18, and you want the property to be sold when you die, you will need to leave clear instructions to the trustees so that they understand your wishes. You will also need to leave instructions about how you wish the money to be distributed to your children. For example, you may ask that the proceeds of sale are used to pay private school fees, or that the money is invested in equities and distributed to your children at various significant stages of their lives (see chapter 12). If you need to bear in mind the needs of a surviving spouse, you can set up a trust that enables him to live in the property until he dies, at which time the property is passed to your children for them to sell according to your wishes (see chapter 12).

Knowing about the Inheritance (Provision for Family and Dependants) Act

The Inheritance (Provision for Family and Dependants) Act 1975, and the Inheritance (Provision for Family and Dependants) Order (Northern Ireland) 1979, entitles certain people to apply to court for 'reasonable financial provision'. This may occur in cases where a spouse, partner, child or other relative feels that he has not been financially provided for when a person has died. This can be in cases where a Will has been made or in cases where the rules of intestacy apply.

The amount considered to be reasonable financial provision varies, depending on who is making the application. In cases involving the deceased's children, it is taken to mean the amount that is required for their maintenance, with the court making decisions based on the present and future financial needs (which will be influenced by the child's age) and the resources of the applicant.

If a court decides that reasonable financial provision has not been made, it can decide to order a lump sum payment from the estate, or periodical payments of an amount and number to be determined by the court. It could also order that property is sold so that payment can be made to the applicant or that property is transferred to the applicant.

For these inheritance rules to apply, the deceased must have had his permanent home in England, Wales or Northern Ireland before he died. In general, an application for reasonable financial provision must be made within six months of obtaining the grant of probate or the letters of administration, although certain claims may be allowed after this time at the discretion of the court. When you plan your estate it is important to think about who might make a claim, and make sure that you plan for this eventuality (see below).

Avoiding claims

As a parent hoping to leave property to your children, you should be aware of any person who may decide to make a claim for reasonable financial provision upon your death as this could have a significant impact on what you are able to leave your children. This is of particular importance if you are divorced or separated, or if there are stepchildren or other children who may have been treated as a member of the family. It is possible to avoid claims under the inheritance rules in three ways:

1   By including a written statement with your Will that states why you have not included provision for a particular person.

2   Through making an official agreement at the time of divorce or separation that states that financial responsibility or provision for a person ends at death.

3   By disposing of property more than six years before your death. However, most people are unable to predict when they are going to die and if you die before six years a court can order the person to whom you gave your property to repay what you gave for the benefit of the person making a claim for reasonable financial provision.

More information about leaving property to your children in cases of separation and divorce is provided in chapter 11 and examples of different divorce and separation scenarios are provided at the end of this book. If you feel that you need to protect your children's inheritance against a person who may try to make a claim for reasonable financial provision, you should seek the advice of a solicitor. To find a specialist solicitor in your area consult the CLS website (www.clsdirect.org.uk) or Law Society website (www.lawsociety.org.uk).

Seeking professional advice

Where inheritance is concerned, circumstances differ for every family. Therefore, it is important to seek the advice of a professional estate planner or financial adviser so that you can maximise your child's inheritance and minimise the problems that he could encounter upon your death. Often, the best way to choose an adviser is on personal recommendation from someone you trust, but you should make sure that he is the right type of adviser for your needs.

When choosing a professional you should make sure that he is regulated by the Financial Services Authority (FSA). You can check that a firm or individual is regulated by the FSA by consulting their register, which can be found at www.moneymadeclear.fsa.gov.uk. If a firm or individual is regulated, you will be able to access the relevant complaints procedures and compensation schemes if things go wrong. You should check that they are also a member of a professional body such as the Society of Will Writers and Estate Planning Practitioners (www.thesocietyofwillwriters.co.uk). Professional bodies ensure that their members are fully trained and qualified to give advice and that they have Professional Indemnity Insurance that will cover you if problems arise.

When you seek specialist professional advice, you need to consider your personal and family circumstances and make sure that you choose the most appropriately trained and qualified professional for your needs. You may need to employ the services of one or more of the following professionals and contact details of a specialist in your area can be obtained from the websites listed below:

- Solicitor (www.lawsociety.org.uk). A solicitor will be able to help with all the legal aspects involved in Wills and probate, transferring property, trusts and tax issues, for example.

- Chartered accountant (www.icaew.co.uk). A chartered accountant will be able to help with tax issues, accounts and filling in self-assessment tax returns. A chartered accountant will be of particular use if you are thinking about setting up a property business as he will be able to look after your accounts and save you money on taxes.

- Trust and estate practitioners or planners (www.step.org). These people will be able to help you to plan your estate, set up trusts and offer advice about tax planning. The terms 'practitioner' and 'planner' tend to be used interchangeably – you just need to make sure that they are fully qualified to offer advice.

- Financial advisers (www.aifa.net) and financial planners (http://professional.financialplanning.org.uk). These people will be able to offer advice about planning your personal finances, obtaining mortgages and investing your money.

- IHT advisers (www.tax.org.uk). These people specialise in offering advice about IHT. These issues can be extremely complex and an experienced adviser should be able to help you save money on this tax.

- Property adviser or surveyor (www.ricsfirms.com). These people will help you to value a property or carry out a survey on a property that you are thinking about buying.

- Investment manager or stockbroker (www.apcims.co.uk). These people will be able to offer advice about the different types of investment such as ISAs, Child Trust Funds and Self-Invested Personal Pensions.

Most of the directories on the websites listed above will enable you to search for a professional by geographical location and specialist area, which include estate planning, IHT, divorce and separation, retirement planning and investment planning.

Discussing inheritance with your children

If your children are old enough to understand the type of investment that you are making on their behalf, you should discuss the pertinent issues with them. This will help them to understand why you have invested your money in property and help them to act according to your wishes once they have inherited the property. Depending on the age of your children you might find it useful to include them in meetings with professionals such as estate planners and financial advisers. If they are old enough to understand the issues, they can ask questions and seek clarification from the adviser so that everyone in the family understands your plans.

If they are too young to understand the issues involved, it is important to discuss your plans with your personal representatives and/or trustees. You may also find it helpful to talk through issues with the people whom you have appointed to look after your children when you die (the guardians). More information about appointing guardians is provided in chapter 11. Often, when you have to explain complex issues to a third party, it helps if you clarify the facts in your own mind first. If anything is unclear at this stage, you must return to your adviser to seek clarification.

It is important to build up a good relationship with your adviser so that you can approach him when required, especially if your family circumstances change. A good adviser should make regular reviews of your circumstances to ensure that your plans remain the most appropriate and the best for your children. He should also make sure that you are fully aware of any forthcoming changes in legislation that may affect your future plans. All changes should be discussed with your children as soon as they are old enough to fully understand.

Author's note

As a family we have decided that we will discuss inheritance issues with all our children when the youngest one becomes a teenager. We feel that they should all be able to understand the issues involved when they have reached their teens, and they will be able to ask questions about their inheritance. It will be interesting for us to talk to them all together as we feel they may have different views about these issues. Although we are going to talk about their plans for the future, and how our property investment will be able to help with these plans, we have decided that we are not going to be specific about the amount of money involved. We feel it is important that our children are able to stand on their own two feet financially and not rely on their inheritance to provide them with a living.

Summary

If you are intending to invest in property for your children, it is important to understand the issues, rules and regulations involved with inheritance. These vary, depending on the age of your children and your family circumstances. If you are separated or divorced, or if there are stepchildren involved, you must make sure that you protect your children against other people who could make a claim on their inheritance. It is important, also, to discuss the issues with your children so that they understand your reasons for investing your money in the manner that you have chosen, and so that they understand how to make the most of your investment when they inherit your property. You can also make sure that arguments are avoided, stress and upset is minimised and the need for expensive solicitors reduced, by filing all the relevant paperwork and instructions with your Will.

An important part of understanding the issues surrounding property inheritance concerns IHT. Details of this tax are discussed in the following chapter.

CHAPTER 3

Understanding Inheritance Tax

All parents who are hoping to leave property to their children must be aware of the Inheritance Tax (IHT) implications during their lifetime and on their death. More and more people are becoming liable to pay this tax as house prices have risen much quicker than the threshold above which IHT is due. Yet there are ways to reduce the IHT bill for children, as long as you undertake careful planning and perhaps seek specialist professional advice.

This chapter helps you to understand more about IHT and the implications for your family, describing what the tax is, how it is paid and offering advice on how to value your assets. It also illustrates how you can give away gifts and assets during your lifetime so that you can help your children financially while you are alive, and reduce their IHT bill upon your death.

Knowing about Inheritance Tax liability

IHT is paid on the estate of a person who has died if the taxable value of his estate is above £312,000 (2008/09 levels). This figure is known as the 'threshold' or 'nil rate band' and it will rise over the next two years to the following levels:

- £325,000 in 2009/10

- £350,000 in 2010/11

The tax is only paid on the part of the estate that is above this limit and this is set at the date of death, not when the estate has been 'settled'. The 'settlement date' is the date by which the executors or administrators have completed their work and all money has been paid to beneficiaries. This date can be several months after the time of death, during which time it is possible for the value of the estate to change. If your estate is worth less than the nil rate band there is no IHT to pay. Currently, the rate of IHT is 40 per cent. As an example, if the value of your estate is £562,000, the threshold is exceeded by £250,000, which means that the IHT payable would be £100,000. Obviously, this is a large amount of money for your children to pay on your death and in many cases it means that children have to sell the family home to be able to pay the tax bill. If you do not want this to happen, it is imperative that you undertake careful and detailed estate planning.

New rules for married couples and civil partners

In October 2007, the Chancellor announced changes that make it possible for spouses or civil partners to add their nil rate band allowance together. This means that there is a total allowance of £624,000 on the first death before IHT is due on the estate and this figure will rise to £700,000 by 2010. This change has been backdated to include estates currently held by widows and widowers.

Before this announcement was made it was possible to make sure that you both made use of the nil rate band, but this could only be done with careful estate planning. Now this change enables married couples and civil partners to simplify the way they distribute their estate on the first death.

UK domiciled residents

Any individual who is domiciled in the UK is liable to IHT on a worldwide basis. This means that, if you own property abroad, and you are domiciled in the UK, IHT will be payable on the property abroad in addition to the assets you have in the UK. 'Domicile' is different to 'residence' in that a person can be resident in more than one country at one time, but can only have one domicile. This is usually the place where a person's permanent home is situated. 'Domicile of origin' is acquired at birth and is the domicile of your father if you were legitimate (i.e. your parents were married to each other) or your mother if you were not. For IHT purposes you can be deemed domiciled in the UK if you have lived for 17 out of the last 20 years in the UK at the time tax is to be calculated, or if you have been UK domiciled for any time in the three years immediately preceding the time at which tax is to be calculated, that is three years before death.

Changing your domicile

It is possible to change your domicile to a 'domicile of choice' from the age of 16 onwards, but you will have to leave your country to settle in another country and provide strong proof that this is a permanent arrangement. If you are deemed to be non-UK domiciled, you only have to pay IHT on chargeable property that you own in the UK. However, you should be aware that there may be tax implications on property that you own in the country in which you are now domiciled and in some circumstances you may be required to pay IHT in both countries. Also, if you change your domicile you will not be able to take advantage of certain trusts that might help you mitigate against IHT (see chapter 12).

Obtaining relevant advice

If you live abroad, or have property abroad, it is essential that you seek professional advice in relation to your tax liability in the UK and in the country in which you own property. This is because inheritance rules differ between countries; for example, Greece and Portugal do not levy inheritance tax on property that is left to close relatives, whereas France and Spain can charge higher tax on property. Also, unlike the UK, France and Spain do not allow assets to pass tax free automatically to spouses on death. It is important to make sure that you have a Will drafted in both the UK and the country in which your property is located as this should help to avoid problems for your children when you die (see chapter 11).

Paying IHT

IHT must be paid within six months of your death and is paid by your personal representative/administrator. IHT on most of the estate, such as investments, pensions, insurance policies, bank accounts and building society accounts, must be paid before probate can be granted. IHT on property and land can be paid in ten annual instalments until the property is sold. However, interest will be charged on any IHT owed after the six-month due date. If you do not want the property to be sold, or you want your children to make their own decisions when they are old enough, you should make sure that their IHT liability can be met without their having to sell the property. This could be done by arranging an appropriate life insurance policy (see chapter 10), by giving away assets and money before you die (see below), or through buying or transferring a property into your child's name when he reaches the age of 18 (see chapter 7).

Understanding Inheritance Tax implications

The Scottish Widows IHT Index reports that almost 9.4 million homeowners will have an estate that will be liable for a 40 per cent tax bill on their death (www.scottishwidows.co.uk). This is 37 per cent of the population in the UK and, if you intend to invest in property for your children and the property is legally owned by you when you die, your estate could be included in this figure. This is because property prices have risen at a far greater rate than the threshold for IHT. The Scottish Widows research points out that, if the IHT threshold had risen at the same rate as house prices, the figure would now reach £419,754. This indicates that successive governments have failed to keep IHT thresholds in line with house price rises since it was introduced by the Conservative government in 1986. In the Pre-Budget Report in October 2007 the Chancellor announced his intention to consider house prices when making future increases in the nil rate band. Even though the threshold is to rise to £350,000 in 2010, it is highly unlikely that the number of people liable to IHT will be reduced, unless we experience a significant property market crash in which property prices are reduced considerably.

Although many more people are now affected by IHT, there has not been a corresponding rise in people seeking advice about how to reduce their liability. There are several reasons for this, including an unwillingness to make arrangements concerning the death of loved ones and a lack of knowledge and understanding about the tax. However, the implications of this lack of planning can be severe, as outlined in the case studies below. Therefore, if you intend to invest in property for your children, you must plan your estate carefully.

CASE STUDY 1 – MARK

Mark is a 32-year-old student studying for a PhD in Chemistry. He is hoping to become a university lecturer on completion of his studies, earning around £21,000 in his first job. However, at present, he has a research grant of £5,000 a year and supplements his income through part-time lecturing, earning £25 an hour.

When Mark started his studies as an undergraduate student at the age of 18 his parents decided to buy him a house to live in while he was studying. It had four bedrooms and his parents let the other rooms to students, making a decent income on the accommodation and enjoying their role as landlords. Mark continued to live in the accommodation after he had completed his undergraduate studies and his parents were happy to continue acting as landlords, especially as house prices and rents were beginning to rise in the area.

Unfortunately, Mark's father died four years later. In his Will he left the family home and the home in which Mark lived to his wife. At the time there was no tax to pay because the properties were left to his wife and property left to a spouse is exempt from IHT.

Mark continued to live in the house with other lodgers and his mother continued to act as landlord until she died this year. As an only child he was left everything in his mother's Will. Over the last decade the prices of both properties had rocketed, resulting in his mother's total estate being worth around £750,000. Mark was shocked to find out that the IHT bill was about £180,000 (based on 2007/08 figures). As a doctoral student on a small research grant with no savings there was no way that Mark could meet this bill without selling one of the properties. He found the choice a horrible one to make – sell the family home in which he had grown up and that his parents had loved and lived in most of their lives, or sell the home where he and his friends had lived for several years. Mark said, 'I don't even think it had crossed my mum's mind to think about this tax. It certainly hadn't occurred to me and I'm supposed to be an intellectual person. In the end I've decided to sell both properties and buy somewhere else – I just couldn't make the choice between the two. It felt like I was being disloyal somehow, whichever decision I made. So I'm going to sell both and now I've been told I've got to think about CGT because I didn't live in one of the houses. Well, I guess these taxes have to be paid but it seems such a shame when Mum and Dad worked so hard to look after me. It's all been so complicated and it's something I just didn't need when I was trying to study and finish my thesis.'

Taking action to reduce Inheritance Tax

As the example above illustrates, it is imperative that, as property owners hoping to leave property to your children, you understand how to reduce IHT. There are several ways you can do this and people choose different methods, depending on their family circumstances.

The Scottish Widows research described above looked into the action that people take to mitigate IHT. Their research produced the following findings:

- making a Will (63%);
- setting up a trust (32%);
- visiting a financial adviser (28%);
- changing joint ownership of a home to tenants in common (28%);
- giving away money (23%).

To plan your estate effectively and make sure that you reduce your children's IHT liability, it is important to seek specialist professional advice when you decide to take any of the action described above. Information and advice about making a Will is discussed in chapter 11. Details about leaving property in trust are provided in chapter 12 and more information about giving away money and making gifts is provided below.

Author's note

Although we have an accountant and a financial manager in our family, we still understand the importance of seeking relevant professional advice. We have a trusted independent financial adviser whom we can turn to whenever we need to – he provides an invaluable service and has saved us considerable amounts of money over the years.

Giving away property and assets

As a parent you can decide to give away your property and assets to your children, either before or after your death. However, you should note that where a gift has been made within seven years before the date of your death the gift must be added to your estate when calculating whether IHT is due, unless the gift is exempt from IHT (see below). Therefore, the recipient of your gift may be liable to IHT on the gift. You can avoid this by mentioning specifically in your Will that all IHT liability should be met from assets held within your estate.

If you decide to make gifts to your children while you are still alive, certain gifts are exempt from IHT liability, even if you die within seven years of making the gift. Examples of such gifts include a sum of up to £3,000 in each tax year, certain wedding gifts and gifts for care and maintenance (see chapter 4). If you want to make larger gifts, such as larger sums of money or a house, they will not be exempt so you will need to take a gamble that you will not die within seven years of having made the gift if you want to avoid IHT. Also, you will need to be aware of other tax that may be payable on larger gifts, such as a house (see chapter 5). This type of gift is called a 'potentially exempt transfer' (PET) because it has the potential to be exempt from IHT if you survive the gift by seven years (see chapter 4).

Taper relief for gifts

If you make a gift and you die before seven years, there is a 'taper relief' that can reduce the tax payable on the gift. This relief is paid only on any assets that were gifted to your children that are above the IHT threshold –

if the gift was not above this threshold, there will be no relief due because there is no tax payable. The reduction in tax is as follows:

- no relief for three years between gift and death;

- 20% between three and four years;

- 40% between four and five years;

- 60% between five and six years;

- 80% between six and seven years.

Gifts with reservation of benefit

Another option you might choose, but which should be approached with extreme caution, is to make a gift to your children from which you can still benefit, such as transferring ownership of your property to your children, yet continuing to live in the property until you die (see case study 2 below).

This type of gift is called a 'gift with reservation of benefit' and, if you are still enjoying a benefit from the gift when you die, your property is treated as part of your estate and will be liable to IHT. You should note, also, that there is no seven-year limit on gifts with reservation of benefit. This type of arrangement has implications for both IHT and CGT. If you dispose of the home in which you live, you do not have to pay CGT because there is an exemption called the Private Residence Relief (PRR), which means that CGT is not payable on your main residence. However, if your children own the home, but do not live in the property, the PRR does not apply and they will be liable to pay CGT if they choose to sell the property when you die. More information about this exemption is provided in chapter 5.

One final point to be aware of is that, once you have given your home away, your children become the owners and it becomes part of their assets. This means that if they become bankrupt your house may have to be sold to pay creditors. Also, if they were to get divorced, your house may have to be sold to fund part of a divorce settlement.

Keeping records

If you make a lifetime gift, it is imperative that you keep records of the gift so that you can present these to the tax officer when requested. You should seek professional advice about how to keep accurate records, but as a general guide the record should include the following:

- your name and address;
- date of the gift;
- name and address of recipient;
- details of the gift;
- information about whether you intend IHT liability to remain with you or be transferred to the recipient, although if the gift is a PET responsibility will be with the recipient (see chapter 4);
- your signature;
- the signature of the recipient;
- name, address, occupation and signature of a witness.

CASE STUDY 2 – ALISON

'When my dad died he left everything to my mum but she wanted to make sure that we were doing all right financially when she was still alive. So she decided to give her house to us – me and my brother – even though she wanted to live in it until she died. We were happy to do this because it meant that Mum could still live in the house and we owned a house that was worth quite a bit of money. It all sounded a bit morbid, but we were happy to go along with it because it was what Mum wanted to do. Mum lived in the house happily for over six years, but then died suddenly of a heart attack. Obviously, it's the worst time of your life having to deal with everything when your mum has died, but to cap it all we had a huge tax bill to pay which neither of us was prepared for.

When everything was added together, including the house, it worked out that we would have to pay around £120,000 IHT. We couldn't believe it. The only way we could get that kind of money was to sell Mum's house, then we found out that we would have to pay CGT on the house because we were not living in it, even though we owned it. It was a nightmare. Neither my brother nor I had much money and my Mum and Dad had spent all their lives trying to build up a good inheritance for us and now the taxman was going to take so much from us.

We had to get financial advice and try to make the best of a really bad situation. In the end the house was sold and we paid all the bills but we were left with almost half the amount Mum and Dad intended. It's certainly made me realise the importance of getting professional advice. My dad thought he understood the rules, but he hadn't really explained these very well to me, my brother or my mum. With hindsight she never should have given the house to us, especially at her age. But at the time we all thought we were doing the right thing.

When my children are old enough I'm going to discuss everything with them and make sure I plan it all carefully with a professional estate planner. Mum and Dad would feel so awful if they knew they had left these kinds of problems. I'm determined not to do that to my kids, however much they annoy me in the meantime!

Valuing your estate

To work out the IHT liability for your children you will need to value your estate. There are several estate valuing tools available on the Internet, such as the IHT Calculator available on the Scottish Widows website (www.scottishwidows.co.uk). However, these tools are only general guides and cannot provide accurate information for individual families. It is important, therefore, to value your own estate accurately and seek professional advice if you feel you cannot undertake the task yourself.

To value your estate you will need to consider the following assets:

Property and chattels:

- your own house;
- other property that you own;
- house contents;
- car(s);
- valuables, such as jewellery, works of art, etc.

Investments:

- PEPS;
- ISAs;
- life assurance policies;
- overseas assets;
- stock exchange investments;
- trusts;
- business assets;
- certain gifts made within the last seven years.

Debts (to be subtracted from the total of the above):

- outstanding mortgage;
- equity release debts;
- loans;
- hire purchase agreements;
- bills;
- unpaid Income Tax;
- bank overdrafts;
- funeral expenses.

Jointly owned assets are normally regarded as being owned fifty-fifty, so the value of any property or chattels that are jointly owned should be halved. You should keep evidence of assets that are jointly owned so that you or your spouse can prove that this is the case if your valuations should be disputed.

When working out the value of your assets it is important to work out the open market values rather than insurance values as insurance values tend to be higher. In certain circumstances it is possible to use an estimated value, rather than an actual value, but you should try to be as accurate as possible so that you can work out the correct IHT figure. Information and advice about working out figures is provided with the relevant IHT forms (see Appendix 6 for a sample IHT 200 form).

There are other issues which you should be aware of when working out the value of property that you have invested for your children. You do not have to obtain a professional valuation, but your valuation should be as accurate as possible. If you are keeping abreast of fluctuations in the property market and you are using your property for investment purposes, this should be fairly easy. You can take into account the state of repair of the property and, if it is in a poor state, this can decrease the value. However, as a property investor your property should not be in a poor state as you or your children could lose out financially on your investment. You will also need to take into account aspects of the property that may increase the value; for example, features that are attractive to builders and developers such as location, size of garden and access to other land.

Relief for loss of sale

If your children or your personal representatives sell an inherited property within four years of the date of death for less than the value on which IHT was paid, they may be able to claim relief for loss of sale. This situation can occur where property prices have fallen in a certain location and will have more relevance with the current unpredictable housing market. More information about claiming this relief can be obtained from the HMRC website (www.hmrc.gov.uk).

Summary

IHT is paid on the estate of a person who has died if the taxable value of their estate is above the threshold. The tax is only paid on the part of the estate that is above this limit and this is set at the date of death. At this present time the rate of IHT is 40 per cent. Depending on the value of your estate, this can be a significant tax liability for your children when you die. However, you can reduce the amount that your children will have to pay through careful planning, by writing a Will, setting up a trust, changing property ownership and seeking appropriate professional advice.

One of the more popular ways to mitigate IHT is to reduce the value of your estate. You can do this by giving money and/or property to your children during your lifetime, making use of all the exemptions, relief and transfers that are available. These are discussed in the following chapter.

CHAPTER 4

Knowing about Inheritance Tax exemptions

IHT is paid on the deceased's estate if the taxable value of his estate is above the IHT threshold at the time of death, as we have seen in the previous chapter. However, not everyone is liable to pay IHT and there are certain gifts and beneficiaries that are exempt from the tax.

As a parent investing in property for your children it is important that you understand, and take advantage of, relevant exemptions. This is because the value of your investment property, and the type of ownership on the property, may mean that your child has a hefty IHT liability on your death. If you reduce your estate by making gifts to your children during your lifetime, you can help them financially while you are alive and reduce their tax bill after your death. You can also reduce their tax liability by making transfers of property to an appropriate trust, either during your lifetime or on your death. The exemptions, gifts and transfers that are relevant to your children and investing in property are described in this chapter.

Exempt gifts

As we saw in the previous chapter, one of the ways that you can reduce your children's IHT liability on your death is to give away money during your lifetime. A number of gifts are exempt from IHT, and as far as your children are concerned, there are several exempt gifts that may be of interest:

- Wedding or civil partnership gifts. Your children can use this gift to put towards the deposit for a house, for example. These gifts should be made before the wedding with the strict proviso that the wedding will actually take place. If the wedding is cancelled, the gift must be returned to you, otherwise there will be IHT implications if the gift exceeds the annual exemption of £3,000 (see below). Remember that you and your spouse can each make the gift. Marriage or civil partnership gifts can be made at the following rates:

    - parents can give £5,000;

    - grandparents and other relatives can each give £2,500;

    - anyone else can give £1,000.

- Small gifts of up to £250 can be made to as many people as you wish in any one tax year, which can include your children, although it cannot be used in conjunction with the annual exemption described below.

- An annual exemption of £3,000 per year. This cannot be used in conjunction with the small gift, but can be given with the wedding/civil partnership gift. This exemption can be carried forward for one year, meaning that you can give £6,000 in one tax year if you did not use your annual exemption in the previous year. As parents you should both remember to make use of your annual exemption. Again, this could be used for your child to put down as a deposit on a house, or for other property-related purposes, such as home improvements or an extension.

- Maintenance gifts of a reasonable amount. Although exact amounts aren't specified you could not give away more than what would be considered necessary for maintenance purposes to the following people:

    - your spouse or civil partner;

    - your ex-spouse or former civil partner;

    - relatives who are dependent on you because they are old or have a disability;

    - your children, which includes adopted or stepchildren, if they are under the age of 18 or in full-time education.

Author's note

I have a friend who, along with her sister, has been given £1,500 a year from her parents for the last five years. My friend has her own children and has been using the money for things that will benefit the kids, such as refurbishing a playroom and paying for swimming and football lessons. Her parents are giving away the money to reduce IHT on their death and they are happy to see that it is also helping their grandchildren while they are alive.

Regular gifts out of income

In addition to the exempt gifts mentioned above, it is possible to make regular gifts that are part of your normal expenditure. These gifts must be made from your after-tax income and should be part of your regular expenditure. Also, after making such gifts you must be left with sufficient income to maintain your normal standard of living. The money must be surplus to your requirements and these gifts must not impoverish you in any way.

In certain cases it can be difficult to convince HM Revenue & Customs that the above conditions have been met, so it is important to keep records of these gifts to prove that you made the payments from your income and not from your capital. As the tax payer, the onus is on you to prove that you have met the required conditions. It is advisable to start giving as soon as possible so that a regular pattern can be put in place. Standing orders from bank accounts over a period of three or more years should be enough to convince the tax officer. Examples of this type of gift that relate to your children include regular premiums of life insurance policies that could be used to meet IHT liability on your death, or private school fees. Also, as parents you could make regular payments into Child Trust Funds or stakeholder pensions for your children (see Appendix 5).

You can give these sums away monthly, annually or as frequently as you wish, and they will not be counted as part of your estate when you die. There is no limit to how much you give, as long as you can prove that it is from your regular income and that the gift does not impoverish you in any way. The gifts do not have to be the same amount each year, but you do need to set up a regular pattern of giving. These gifts can be made in addition to the other types of exempt gift described above.

Potentially exempt transfers

The gifts listed above are all exempt gifts for IHT purposes. Most other gifts that you make during your lifetime are described as 'potentially exempt transfers' (PETs). They are potentially exempt because, if you survive the gift by seven years, your beneficiaries will not have to pay IHT on the gift. However, if you die before the seven years, the gift is treated as a chargeable transfer and is not exempt from IHT. (A chargeable transfer is a gift or other transfer of value made by an individual which is not covered by any of the various exemptions and which is therefore a transfer for IHT purposes.) If the gift was greater than the IHT threshold, currently £312,000, there is some tax relief available, called taper relief (see chapter 3 for current levels of relief). It is possible for you to take out a seven-year term assurance policy that would cover potential liability on your death within seven years. This is called a 'gift inter vivos policy' and the cover decreases in line with the diminishing IHT liability. If this policy is set up in trust, it will ensure that the funds fall outside your estate for IHT purposes. More information about life assurance is provided in chapter 10 and different scenarios for making gifts and reducing IHT are provided at the end of this book.

Gifts that count as a PET include the following:

- gifts to your child or grandchild;
- a trust for someone who is disabled (a minor or adult child);
- a bereaved minor's trust (when certain conditions are met, such as a surviving parent has decided to transfer their right to receive anything from the trust to their child). More information about this type of trust is provided in chapter 12.

Only gifts that have been made outright count as a PET. If a gift has been made with strings attached, it is called a 'gift with reservation of benefit'. This type of gift was described in chapter 3.

Downsizing to a smaller property

Some parents decide that they wish to downsize to a smaller property and give the proceeds of the sale to their children. If you want to take this course of action, you should be aware that you will need to make the gifts in the manner described above; for example, you could choose to use your annual exemption and make gifts of £3,000 each year over a set period of time or until all the money has been given away. This figure could rise to £12,000 in the first year if you did not use your annual exemption in the previous year and both parents add their annual exemptions together.

Alternatively, you could choose to use your annual exemption of £3,000 (or £6,000 for both of you) and give a larger sum as a PET. This would mean that the larger gift would be exempt from IHT if you were to survive the gift by seven years.

Finally, if your son or daughter is about to get married, both parents can make a wedding gift of £5,000 each and an annual exempt gift of £3,000 each. This would enable you to give your child a total gift of £16,000 (£22,000 if you have not used your annual exemption in the previous year) which will be free of IHT. This is a useful way to give away money that you have made by downsizing your property without affecting your children's IHT liability. Your children could use this money to put down a deposit on a house, or, if they are already homeowners, for home improvements. If your children are still young, you can make use of IHT exemptions to invest the money on their behalf (see Appendix 5) or consider buying a second property with the proceeds (see chapter 9).

Chargeable lifetime transfers

Children cannot legally own land and buildings until they are 18 so trusts are a useful way to leave property to minor children. A trust is a legal entity in its own right – when a trust owns a property it belongs to the trust rather than to you, as the person who set up the trust. Trustees are the people who control and maintain the trust, making sure that the income and assets are passed to the beneficiaries in the manner that you wish. They can also be used to help you reduce the IHT liability on your death (see chapter 12 for information about the different types of trust). As a property investor you may choose to make a gift of land and buildings to a trust that can be used to safeguard your investment for your children.

When you make a gift of property into a trust during your lifetime it is neither an exempt gift nor a PET, but instead is a chargeable lifetime transfer (CLT). This is because, if the amount of gift (or the value of the property) exceeds the IHT threshold of £312,000 (2008/09 levels), IHT of 20 per cent is immediately payable on any amount in excess of this threshold. If you die within seven years of making this transfer, the assets are brought back into your estate and will be included when IHT is calculated. However, the fact that 20 per cent IHT has already been paid will be taken into account when the IHT bill is calculated, thus reducing your children's IHT liability on your death.

You should note, however, that 20 per cent IHT is only charged on any transfer into a trust that is over the IHT threshold of £312,000. Therefore, you can choose to transfer a property into a trust for your children and, if the value is less than this threshold, there will be no IHT payable when you make the transfer. However, if the value of the property rises above the threshold, the trustees will face a ten-year-anniversary charge and exit charges when capital leaves the trust. More information about these charges is provided in chapter 12. Also, you should note that if the trustees have a potential IHT liability on your death within seven years of making the gift into the trust, they can consider insuring your life under a seven-year term assurance policy. As premiums of this nature can be hefty if you are older or considered to be high risk, it may be preferable for them to be met from trust monies, rather than by you, as the insured.

Making the most of exemptions, relief and transfers

As we have seen in chapter 3, if you are investing in property for your children, and the property is in your name when you die, your children could face a large IHT bill, especially if you have more than one property and other assets to leave to them. However, there are steps that you can take to reduce this bill, as detailed below. This could mean the difference between your children being able to hold onto the investment property, or being forced to sell in order to raise the appropriate finances to pay their tax bill.

- Make sure that you make maximum use of all exemptions and relief during your lifetime (see above). You can give a certain amount of money each year to your children and they could use this to build up a deposit to buy their own house, for example. This would mean that the value of your estate would be reduced when IHT is calculated on your death, yet, in effect you are still investing in property for your child by helping him onto the property ladder.

- Make full use of the current IHT threshold by making a chargeable lifetime transfer up to the threshold and a potentially exempt transfer above this amount (see above), if you believe you will survive the gift by seven years.

- Make sure you write a Will and that it fully utilises the IHT threshold (see chapter 11).

- Set up a discretionary trust in your Will (see chapter 12). This is a low cost, low risk arrangement that leaves the surviving spouse in control of assets and savings. For example, you could set up a discretionary trust that enables your spouse to maintain control of the property until he dies, when the property then passes to the children. If your children are under the age of 18 when your spouse dies, the trustees will maintain and manage the property in the way that you or your spouse has specified.

- Look into the use of insurance to cover the full IHT liability on your death (see chapter 10). For example, you could put £3,000 a year into a life policy. This amount would be covered by your basic IHT exemptions and if the policy is set up under trust, any proceeds should be outside your estate. This would generate a useful sum to meet IHT bills on your death as well as reducing the value of your estate. This means that your children would have their IHT liability covered and would not need to sell the family home to pay the tax, for example.

- If your children are over the age of 18, you could think about buying a property in their name. However, if the gift were to exceed the exempt amount described above, you would have to survive the gift by seven years so that it is not added back to your estate for IHT purposes. If you were to survive the gift by seven years, there would be no IHT liability on this property upon your death as you do not own the property. There would also be no CGT liability if your child made the property his main home (see chapters 5 and 7).

- Make sure that your arrangements are flexible and can adapt to changing circumstances.

- Seek specialist advice.

Summary

As a property investor hoping to leave a good inheritance for your children, it is important that you understand, and make use of, the different types of IHT exemption. These include annual gifts of £3,000, small gifts of £250 and wedding gifts of £5,000. Also, it is possible to make gifts to your children that are potentially exempt from IHT, if you survive the gift by seven years. Transfers into trusts during your lifetime are called chargeable lifetime transfers, and there is an immediate charge to IHT on this type of transfer. Through careful planning and by making use of all exemptions, reliefs and transfers, you can reduce the IHT liability for your children when you die.

If you are hoping to invest in property for your children, there are a number of other property taxes which you should be aware of, as these could reduce the amount of money that your children inherit. These issues are discussed in the following chapter.

CHAPTER 5

Paying other tax on property

There are a variety of other taxes, in addition to IHT, that may be payable on property transactions. Some of these are upfront taxes payable when you buy a property, whereas others are payable on rental income, services and goods or when you dispose of a property. It is important to be aware of these taxes when planning your property investment as some of them may have serious financial implications that may make your investment less financially sound than alternative types of investment.

The taxes that you could be liable to pay are discussed in this chapter. This will help you to work out how much you have to pay before you choose to make your property investment, and alert you to taxes that may be payable by your children when they inherit your property upon your death.

Stamp Duty Land Tax

Stamp Duty Land Tax (SDLT) replaced Stamp Duty in 2003 and is payable on the purchase of land and buildings in the UK. However, it is only payable on residential properties costing more than £125,000 and there is relief available for transactions in disadvantaged areas. You can find out if a property you are interested in qualifies for Disadvantaged Areas Relief (DAR) by using the search tool available on the HMRC website (www.hmrc.gov.uk). You will need the postcode of the property to use the search tool. If you do not know the postcode, you can find out by visiting the Royal Mail website (www.royalmail.com) or telephoning the Postcode Helpline on 0845 711 1222.

Current SDLT rates are provided in Table 3 below. For up-to-date rates visit the HMRC website (www.hmrc.gov.uk).

TABLE 3: STAMP DUTY LAND TAX RATES (2008/09)

Rates	Residential Land in Disadvantaged Areas	All Other Residential Land in the UK	All Other Non-Residential Land in the UK
zero	£0 – £150,000	£0 – £125,000	£0 – £150,000
1%	Over £150,000 – £250,000	Over £125,000 – £250,000	Over £150,000 – £250,000
3%	Over £250,000 – £500,000	Over £250,000 – £500,000	Over £250,000 – £500,000
4%	Over £500,000	Over £500,000	Over £500,000

As the buyer of a property you are responsible for ensuring that SDLT is paid, although in practice the paperwork is usually arranged by your solicitor or conveyancer. Since the buyer remains liable for the information submitted to HMRC and for the tax due you will need to make sure that all the information supplied on the SDLT tax return form is correct before you sign the declaration that is printed on it.

When deciding to invest in property for your children, SDLT can add a significant amount to the costs of a house purchase so you will need to take account of this tax when you plan your budget (see chapter 6). Also, you should note that if you decide to help your child onto the property ladder by taking out a joint mortgage, there may be SDLT implications for your child if he decides to buy your share of the property at a later date, depending on the value of the property (see chapter 7). This is also the case if you decide to transfer a property that you have bought in your name to your child's name when he reaches the age of 18.

Capital Gains Tax

Capital Gains Tax (CGT) is paid on gains made from selling or disposing assets, which includes residential and business property. This tax is only payable where an asset has increased in value since you acquired it and you will not have to pay any CGT if your total gains are less than the annual exempt amount, which is £9,600 in 2008/09. Also, there are a number of allowances, reliefs and elections that can reduce the amount of CGT that you have to pay.

In April 2008 a flat rate of 18 per cent was introduced for individuals, trustees and personal representatives on taxable gains. For up-to-date policy information, current figures and to obtain information about reporting gains or losses, visit the HMRC website (www.hmrc.gov.uk).

Private Residence Relief

When you sell your main home you don't have to pay CGT as this qualifies for the Private Residence Relief (PRR) exemption. However, it is payable on any other residential property that is not your main home, such as rental property or inherited property. For a property to be defined as your main home, it must meet the following conditions:

- the house was purchased primarily for your main home and was not bought solely for profit;

- the property was your own home throughout the time you have owned it (ignoring the last three years of ownership – this is because the final 36 months of ownership of a property attracting PRR are always exempt from CGT, even if you are renting it out);

- the property was used as your own home and not let to tenants, although one lodger living in the family home is permissible;

- the building and grounds that are to be sold do not exceed 5,000 square metres;

- you do not have extensive outbuildings;

- you have not used any part of the property solely for business purposes.

If you (or your children if they are disposing of a property that they have inherited) do not meet these conditions, CGT may be chargeable. However, it is possible to reduce the CGT amount through deducting some of the costs of buying, selling and improving the property. Also, you should note that if the property has made a loss rather than a gain, it is possible to set the loss against other chargeable gains you may have on other assets.

As a parent hoping to leave property to your children you must realise that if you leave your property to your children in your Will, or if you decide to give the property to them while you are alive, and the property is not their main home, CGT will be chargeable if they decide to sell at a later date. As house prices have risen so much over recent years this can be quite a significant tax bill for your children. However, if your children inherit a property and they decide to make it their main home and they meet the conditions described above, there will be no CGT to pay, although they may still have to pay IHT (see chapter 3). As with IHT, there is no CGT payable on transfers between spouses and civil partners.

Pre-Owned Asset Tax

In the Finance Act 2004 the government attempted to close loopholes and stop people setting up schemes that enabled them to avoid gift with reservation of benefit provisions, yet still live in a property without paying rent. This resulted in the introduction of Pre-Owned Asset Tax (POAT), which is an Income Tax charge on the donor who benefits from the gift (this will be you, if you have made a gift to your children).

The legislation is retrospective and applies to an asset that has been given away since 17 March 1986, where the donor continues to use it, but the transaction is not treated as a gift with reservation of benefit (see chapter 3). For example, if you decided to make a gift of money to your child so that your child could buy a house, and then you moved into that house within seven years of the gift being made but do not pay rent, POAT would apply. This is an Income Tax charge on the rent that you should be paying (but that you are not paying). It is possible to avoid this tax by paying a full market rent, although your children will be liable to pay Income Tax instead of your paying POAT (see below). You may find it useful to visit a financial adviser to find out what would be the best course of action.

In the case of land and buildings the POAT will be payable on the open market rental value for that property (this rental value is worked out following a complex formula). However, there is a minimum figure of £5,000 that has been put in place, so if the rental value for the year is less than this amount, you (as the person benefiting from the gift) will not have to pay any tax. Married couples and civil partners can each take advantage of this £5,000 annual exemption before tax is payable, but unused exemptions cannot be transferred between partners.

You should note, however, that if the rental value is above this exempt amount, tax will be payable on the whole figure, not just the excess. For example, if a higher rate taxpayer lives in a property with a rental value of £10,000 a year, he will have an additional tax bill of £4,000 a year (40 per cent of £10,000) and will be unable to take advantage of the annual exemption. Even if the rental value is worth only a small amount above the annual exemption, such as £5,100, you will still have to pay tax on the whole amount. Note that it is you, as the person benefiting from the gift, and not your children who is responsible for paying this tax. This is because you will be living in your child's house, but not paying any rent.

Alternatives to paying POAT

You can choose alternatives to paying this tax, such as opting for a gift with reservation of benefit, although this means that IHT will be chargeable and that the gift will be added to your estate for IHT purposes, regardless of how long you survive the gift, because you are still enjoying the benefit of the gift.

Alternatively, you could choose to pay an open market rent for living in the property. In this case your children will become your landlord and they will be liable to pay tax on the rental income when you choose this option (see below). You would need to decide whether you want to pay your children a full rent and have them pay tax, or whether you would prefer to pay no rent to your children, but instead pay the POAT yourself. You should note also, that if you tried to pay a rent that is less than the full market value, you will be taxed on the balance between what you have paid and what you should be paying.

CASE STUDY 3 – ANNE

Mrs Jackson sold her family home when her husband died and gave the proceeds to her daughter, Anne. Anne wanted to invest the money wisely, so she decided to buy a detached bungalow in which her mother could live. This gave Anne peace of mind because her mother had recently been widowed and Anne could keep an eye on her to check that she was all right.

They both decided that Mrs Jackson would not pay rent as she had given a large sum of money to her daughter. However, they soon found that Mrs Jackson would have to pay tax on the rent that she should have been paying to Anne. The rental value on the bungalow was worked out at £8,340 a year. As a higher rate tax payer, Mrs Jackson was shocked to find that she had to pay an extra £3,336 a year (40 per cent of £8,340) on top of her Income Tax bill. However, if she chose not to pay this tax, she would have to pay £8,340 a year to her daughter, as this was deemed to be the full rental value of the bungalow.

After discussion, Anne felt that it was better for her mother to pay the tax because this was less money for her mother to pay each year, even if it did go straight to the tax man.

Alternative courses of action

As Mrs Jackson was adamant that she sold her family home and give the proceeds to her daughter during her lifetime, her choices were limited. Mrs Jackson could have sold her house, given the money to her daughter, hoped that she survived the gift by seven years and then rented a smaller flat on which she would pay less rent. However, the rent would have to have been below £64 a week if she wanted to pay less money than the POAT she was paying (£64 x 52 weeks = £3,328 in rent, compared to £3,336 POAT). This is a risky strategy because Mrs Jackson may die early, in which case the gift would be added to her estate for IHT purposes. Also, she may have to move to a less desirable flat or area and would not own her own property.

Alternatively, Mrs Jackson could have downsized by buying a smaller property and given an amount of money to her daughter each year within the annual IHT exemption. This would have reduced the value of her estate, enabled her to give gifts of money to her daughter during her lifetime, yet still enabled her to live in a property that she owned in an area that she liked.

Council Tax

When investing in property for your children, there are several issues to be aware of in relation to Council Tax:

- One Council Tax bill is sent to the property regardless of how many people live in the dwelling. A dwelling is defined as a separate unit of living accommodation, together with any garden, yard, garage or other outbuildings attached to it, all occupied by the same person(s) and within the same area of land. If a property contains more than one self-contained unit of accommodation, it will be divided into as many dwellings as there are self-contained units for Council Tax purposes.

- If you let your investment property, your tenants are responsible for paying the Council Tax. However, students will not have to pay the tax, provided that the house is solely occupied by students. This is important if you are thinking about buying an investment property for your child while he is studying, as, if you decide to let other rooms in the house to working people, your child may have to contribute towards the Council Tax bill (see chapter 8).

- If you have bought an investment property and it is empty because it is not yet fit for habitation, you may not have to pay Council Tax on the property. Rules and regulations vary, so contact your local authority for information specific to your locality.

More information about Council Tax can be obtained from the Valuation Office Agency (www.voa.gov.uk). Also, you can find out the Council Tax band of an investment property in which you are interested on this website.

Paying tax on rental income

If you decide to let your investment property, you will be liable to pay tax on your net income from rents. However, you can deduct your day-to-day running expenses and various other expenses from this income. This includes the following:

- property maintenance and repairs;

- letting agent's fees;

- interest on mortgages;

- advertising and marketing costs;

- insurance costs;

- administration, including office and IT costs;

- travel, including motor expenses.

In 2008/09 the taxable bands and rates of Income Tax are as follows:

- Basic rate (22%)   £0 – £34,800

- Higher rate (40%)   over £34,800

If you are married or in a civil partnership, you should remember to both take advantage of your personal allowance, which is £6,035 in 2008/09. You will need to keep all records of income and expenditure and complete a self-assessment tax return each year. Also, you should note that if you let property abroad, you may have to pay UK tax on the rental income if you're resident in the UK for tax purposes (see chapter 9 for more information about buying a property abroad). More information about Income Tax can be obtained from the government information website (www.direct.gov.uk) or from the HMRC website (www.hmrc.gov.uk).

Reducing your tax bill

When trying to reduce your tax bill it is imperative that you keep all paperwork that relates to the buying, selling and improvement of your property. This is because you can claim reductions and relief based on these costs, which include legal fees, SDLT and capital costs, but you will have to prove that you made this expenditure. If you have to fill in a tax return, you will find this easier and quicker to do if you have all the dates and figures easily to hand. People who are self-employed are required to keep all records for five years and limited companies and partnerships are required to keep all records for six years (see chapter 6). Through keeping accurate and well-organised records you will be able to make a claim for overpayment or prove your income and expenditure if cases of dispute should arise.

Also, it is important that you use all the relief and exemptions that are available to you, and make sure that you take advantage of individual allowances that are available to husbands, wives and civil partners. For example, when working out your CGT bill every individual receives a CGT annual allowance, currently £9,600 (2008/09 figures). You and your spouse or civil partner can both take advantage of this, which means that you can reduce the amount of any gain subject to tax by £19,200.

Finally, you can make considerable savings through careful financial planning and by using the services of a professional. Although you will have to pay the professional for his services, he should be able to save you considerable amounts of money by showing you how to take advantage of tax reliefs and exemptions. More information about contacting a professional is provided in chapter 3.

Author's note

We are lucky to have a chartered accountant and financial manager in the family. They know how to make the most of tax reliefs and exemptions. If you don't have this expertise, you really should seek professional advice. My brothers have managed to save us thousands of pounds over the years. Also, they understand tax issues and know how to fill in the forms – it makes life much easier for the rest of us, and saves all the grief associated with filling in complex forms.

Summary

If you are hoping to invest in property for your child, it is important that you understand the tax implications, both for you and for your child. This will help you to make the best investment decisions for your personal and family circumstances. Taxes that you will need to consider include SDLT, CGT, POAT, Council Tax, Income Tax, VAT and tax on rental income. You can reduce your tax bill, and that of your child, through careful planning and by making use of all exemptions, reliefs and individual allowances. An accountant will help you to do this if you do not have the required skills and knowledge.

Once you understand the tax implications on your property investment, it is important to consider your present and future family finances. A careful assessment of your finances will help you to decide whether property investment is suitable for you and your family. These issues are discussed in the following chapter.

CHAPTER 6

Planning your finances

If you are hoping to invest in property, you need to undertake a careful assessment of your finances. This will enable you to decide whether property investment is possible, practical and the best option for you and your family.

When you plan your finances, you need to think about the financial viability of your plans and the impact this type of investment will have on your children and their inheritance. You will also need to think about how you are going to raise the capital for your investment, whether this is through loans, grants or incentive schemes, and how you intend to make sure that your finances are protected. These issues are discussed in this chapter.

Assessing the financial viability of your property investment

When assessing the financial viability of your property investment ideas, you need to ask yourself the following questions:

1   Am I in a secure financial position?

2   Do I have spare capital to invest? If not, can I raise the appropriate capital? Is it prudent to do so? Will my age influence my ability to raise capital?

3 Do I have money that is easily accessible for emergencies and other expenses?

4 Is investing in property the most appropriate type of investment for me and my family? Do I have a thorough understanding of alternative types of investment? (More information about the different types of investment that are available for your child is provided in Appendix 5.)

5 Are market conditions right for investing in property?

6 Can I afford to tie up large sums of money in property investment?

7 Can I find the right property, at the right price, in the right location at the right time?

8 Do I have enough money to buy the right type of property?

9 Am I likely to make money on my investment?

10 Do I understand how the market might change in the future, over both the short and long term? How will this affect my investment? Will I lose money? Can I weather fluctuations in the market? Is my investment flexible enough to withstand short-term fluctuations?

11 How can I protect my investment?

12 How will a change in family circumstances, such as a birth, death or divorce, affect my investment? How can I protect against financial loss in these circumstances?

13 Will investing in property influence my chances of obtaining a mortgage at a later date?

14 Can I continue to meet mortgage payments if I should lose my job through redundancy or ill health?

15 Can I afford to keep a property if I am unable to find tenants for the whole year or if they refuse to pay their rent?

16 Do I understand the potential costs of tenant-related problems?

17 Do I have enough capital to maintain and develop the property as required?

Before you invest in property you need to make sure that you are in a secure financial position. Too many investors rush into an inappropriate investment, believing that there are large profits to be made with little work involved. However, this is not the case. People who invest in property successfully work very hard to keep their investment viable, and they make sure that they are in a secure financial position before they make their investment.

They also realise the importance of setting up a contingency fund for unexpected costs. This fund should be 15–20 per cent of your total investment budget and should be placed in an instant access, high interest savings account until it is needed. Once you have used money from your contingency fund, you should top it up whenever you can.

Author's note

My two eldest brothers bought their first property together as they were able to obtain a better mortgage deal and were able to pool their savings for a contingency fund. The property was dilapidated, but one of my brothers worked hard to make it habitable, using around 90 per cent of the contingency fund on labour and materials. They let this property and were able to buy another, based on their earnings, rental income and the value of the property. My sister and I were invited to join the investment when we had enough capital to offer. My younger brother joined a few years later when he was also able to offer enough capital. We have never overstretched ourselves financially, as we understand that the property market can be unpredictable.

Producing a profit/loss plan and cash flow forecast

All potential investors should produce a profit/loss plan and a cash flow forecast, especially if they hope to raise finance through external backers. All banks, building societies or other lenders will want to see that you have a thorough understanding of your expected income and expenditure and that you are able to work out how your investment will perform, financially, in the future.

Many investments fail because they are undercapitalised and you need to make sure that this is not the case with your investment by producing comprehensive plans and forecasts before you buy your investment property. This is of particular importance if you are hoping to make a living from your property investment and you are thinking about setting up a property company, as we have done with Dawson Properties Ltd. If you are intending to set up a limited company for your property business, you must produce a profit/loss account for each financial year. Self-employed sole traders and most partnerships don't need to produce a formal profit/loss account each year, although you will need to complete an annual self-assessment tax return.

When producing your profit/loss plan and cash flow forecast, you must do so on realistic estimates. These will be based on your market research, personal judgement and assumptions. If you are unable to do this, you should seek professional advice or enrol on a relevant business course. For more information about producing a profit/loss plan and a cash flow forecast visit the Business Link website (www.businesslink.gov.uk). For information about business courses in your area, visit www.learndirect.co.uk.

Working out your budget

In addition to producing a profit/loss plan and cash flow forecast you will need to work out your budget, both in terms of start-up costs and in terms of the day-to-day management of your investment property. When you buy a property there are a number of initial costs that must be paid upfront and you will need to make sure that you have enough capital, or can raise enough capital, to cover these costs. These include the following:

- **The price of the property:** this will vary greatly, depending on the type, size, standard and location. However, you must undertake careful research to make sure that you are obtaining the best price and be prepared to bargain and negotiate to obtain the best deal.

- **SDLT:** this is a percentage of the purchase price and can be a significant amount on more expensive properties. An SDLT calculator is available at http://sdcalculator.inlandrevenue.gov.uk. This is a useful tool to help you to work out how much you would have to pay on your chosen property, whether residential, non-residential or in a disadvantaged area. More information about SDLT is provided in chapter 5.

- **Solicitor's/conveyancer's fees:** these vary, but could be in the range of £600–£1,200. To find a solicitor in your area visit www.lawsociety.org.uk. To find a licensed conveyancer in your area use the online directory at www.conveyancer.org.uk.

- **Surveyor's fees:** some vendors will include a Home Condition Report in their Home Information Pack, although this is not a compulsory component of the pack. In most cases it is advisable to commission your own survey for the property as this can alert you to potential and costly problems. Prices vary, depending on the type of survey and size of property, but should be in the region of £300–£1,000. To obtain contact details of a surveyor in your area use the online directory at www.ricsfirms.com.

- **Mortgage fees:** in most cases you will need to pay an administration fee, which could be in the region of £100–£500. Also, if you decide to use a mortgage broker you may have a fee of up to £300 to pay, although some will receive commission from the mortgage company instead of a fee from its client. In some cases you may have to pay a re-inspection fee if the mortgage company withholds some of your loan until you carry out agreed repairs to the property. This could be up to £250. Contact your chosen lender for more information about their fees.

- **Deposit:** this will need to be paid when you exchange contracts and the amount of deposit will depend on the purchase price, your available funds and the agreement you have made with your mortgage company. If you decide to buy at auction, you will need to have the deposit available on the day if you are successful in your bidding. This will be 10 per cent of the purchase price or a specified minimum sum.

- **Renovation/refurbishment costs:** these will vary depending on the amount and type of work required on the property. You may need to budget for labour, materials, equipment, plant hire, fixtures, fittings, furnishings, decoration, removal and storage.

- **Administration:** you may need to purchase computer hardware and software, such as monitors, printers, fax machines and accountancy packages.

Once you have budgeted for your upfront costs, you need to think about your running costs. These include the following:

- **Mortgage repayments and interest:** these will need to be paid every month and can rise or fall during the loan term, depending on the type of mortgage you take out and the interest rate payable. To check the Bank of England base rate visit www.bankofengland.co.uk.

- **Insurance:** this is essential to your investment and costs should not be reduced by neglecting to take out or taking out inadequate insurance. This is one of the best ways to protect your investment and careful research should be undertaken to obtain the best and most suitable deals (see chapter 10).

- **Administration:** this can include the cost of stationery, contract preparation and postage.

- **Marketing and advertising:** if you are intending to let your property to tenants you will need to budget for advertising costs, which can include advertisements in the local newspaper or the design of a website.

- **Transport:** if you live away from the property you will need to budget for transport costs.

- **Maintenance:** if you are intending to let your property you will need to budget for general maintenance, such as repairs and decoration, and you will need to budget for cleaning and the replacement of items that have been broken or stolen. If you intend to use a letting agent or property management company, ask for a complete breakdown of costs involved so that you can be sure that there will be no hidden extras for which you have not budgeted.

- **Utilities:** you may need to pay initial set-up charges and any other bills that you have agreed to pay.

- **Tax:** you will need to make sure that you have enough money set aside each year to pay your tax bill.

You can use the Financial Services Authority (FSA) budget calculator to work out whether you will have enough income to meet your monthly payments (www.moneymadeclear.fsa.gov.uk). It is imperative that you do not overstretch yourself financially as this will help to protect your investment against slumps in the housing market or future interest rate rises.

Assessing the financial implications for your children

When assessing the financial implications of your investment decisions for your children, you should take note of the following points:

- Make sure that your children are not saddled with your mortgage payments on the investment property if you should die unexpectedly. This can be done by arranging adequate life assurance that makes sure the mortgage is paid on your death (see chapter 10).

- If you decide to take advantage of local authority loan or grant schemes, make sure that your children do not have to pay back the money on your death. These schemes are available for homeowners, landlords and property developers who are interested in buying empty or dilapidated properties that they intend to do up and let to tenants (see below).

- There is no point making sure that your investment works well during your lifetime if you neglect what happens to your investment when you die. You should plan your estate carefully so that you can reduce the IHT and CGT liability for your children on your death (see chapters 3, 4 and 5). The most important part of estate planning is to make sure that you have an appropriate and up-to-date Will. These issues are discussed in chapter 11. For more information about estate planning and to find a practitioner in your area, contact the Society of Trust and Estate Practitioners (STEP) (www.step.org).

- Make sure that you undertake a regular review of your estate and your finances, especially if any of the following situations should arise:

  - the birth of a child or grandchild;

  - separation, divorce, marriage or second marriage of you or your children;

  - if you establish a new property business or buy a new property for investment purposes;

  - a substantial increase or decrease in the value of your estate;

  - the death of your spouse, a potential executor or potential children's guardian;

  - relevant changes in tax law.

Children and tax

Children are generally treated as individuals for the purposes of Income Tax, with the same personal allowance as adults (£6,035 in 2008/09). As with adults, depending on their income they may or may not become tax payers. If their total taxable income is less than the Income Tax personal allowances, you can complete form R85 for them so that they receive interest from savings accounts with no tax taken off. This form can be downloaded from the government website (www.direct.gov.uk) or is available from your bank or building society. They also have to pay CGT, again, having the same allowance as adults (£9,600 in 2008/09).

However, special rules apply to children's savings accounts, ISAs and other investments that you make for them, such as stocks, shares and bonds if they consist of gifts from parents and the income from all of the gifts from each parent adds up to more than £100 in a year. If this is the case, this income will be treated as the parents' and it is you, as the parent, therefore, that will be taxed on this income. The £100 rule applies to your children until they reach 18 or marry (whichever comes first). Income Tax on rental income for an investment property will depend on whether it is you or your child who owns the property and is acting as landlord, and also whether you or your child is a resident landlord (see chapter 8 for more information). You will need to take these issues into account when planning your finances and thinking about the types of investment you wish to take out for your child. More information about alternative types of investment and the tax that will have to be paid is provided in Appendix 5.

Raising capital

You can raise capital for your property investment from a variety of places. These include banks and mortgage companies and local authority grants and loans.

Banks and mortgage companies

You can choose to approach banks and mortgage companies direct, or you can seek advice through an independent financial adviser. Only firms and their agents who are authorised by the FSA can give advice about mortgages and they must follow certain procedures when doing this; for example, under FSA rules you should be provided with a key facts document called 'About this mortgage', which summarises the features and costs of the mortgage which you are interested in. You can check that a firm or agent is authorised by visiting the FSA website (www.fsa.gov.uk). On this site you can use its comparative tool to compare mortgages from different companies and use the mortgage calculator to work out how much your monthly mortgage payments are likely to be. The information provided is for guidance purposes only, but it is useful as a starting point for your mortgage product research.

Buy-to-let mortgages

Buy-to-let mortgages are available for property investors who wish to let their property. The mortgage lender will want to know the letting and income potential of the property, rather than your personal income, so again it is important to produce a profit/loss plan and cash flow forecast. Although terms and conditions vary between lenders, in general you will need to prove that the rental income will provide an annual yield of more than 8 per cent of the mortgage, put down a minimum 15 per cent deposit (this could be larger on certain types of property) and own a main residence.

You should note that some lenders will be reluctant to offer a buy-to-let mortgage on ex-council property, a flat above a shop or in a high-rise block. Also, some have recently begun to refuse applications for buy-to-let mortgages on new-build city centre flats as the market, in some areas, is saturated and investors are finding that they are losing money, both on the capital they have invested and on rental income. Therefore, if you are hoping to obtain a buy-to-let mortgage, it is advisable to find out whether you would be able to obtain a mortgage before making an offer to buy a property.

The recent credit crunch has meant that it is harder to obtain buy-to-let mortgages, although there are still competitive deals available. However, to obtain these deals you will have to put down a larger deposit, work hard to prove that you can meet mortgage payments from the rental yield, and prove that you are in a secure financial position. You will also have to show that you have thoroughly researched the market and that tenants will be available and willing to pay the rent that you require. These are all important issues and should be undertaken regardless of whether the UK is experiencing a credit crunch, if your venture is to succeed. More information about buy-to-let mortgages can be obtained from the Council of Mortgage Lenders' website (www.cml.org.uk).

CAT standard mortgages

The government 'CAT standard' is awarded to mortgages which it considers offer the customer reasonable charges, easy access and fair terms. All advertising and paperwork must be 'straightforward, fair and clear' and the mortgages should be easy for borrowers to understand. Although a CAT standard mortgage is not a government recommendation it is a useful benchmark against which to compare other deals. There are two CAT standards:

1   one for a loan charging variable interest rates;
2   one for a loan which begins with a period when the interest rate is either fixed or subject to an upper limit (capped).

CAT standards for mortgages are voluntary and are not guaranteed to suit every borrower. As they may not be the best deal available, you will need to shop around to find out whether there is anything that is more appropriate for your needs and circumstances. More information about CAT standards for mortgages can be obtained from www.hm-treasury.gov.uk or from your chosen lender.

Local authority grants and loans

There are a number of local authority grants and loans available for homeowners, property developers and landlords, especially if you are interested in buying dilapidated or empty properties to renovate, refurbish and to let to tenants. Examples of the type of schemes on offer include:

- **Home Energy Efficiency Grants:** these grants are available to help owner-occupiers, landlords and tenants to install energy efficient heating and insulation. The grants are means-tested and available to homeowners and tenants who are on means-tested benefits or low incomes. Landlords are not means-tested, but only receive a percentage of the cost of works. If you are interested in making energy efficiency improvements to your property, contact the Energy Saving Trust for information about grants (www.energysavingtrust.org.uk).

- **Renovation Grants:** these are designed to help owner-occupiers carry out repairs or improvements to their properties. In most cases these grants are discretionary and will depend on the amount of funds available. Contact your local authority for more information about these grants.

- **Empty Property Grants:** these grants are available to help people interested in restoring an empty property. The amount of grant you will receive depends on a number of factors, including the type and size of property, its location and the intended use once the work is complete. Some local authorities will specify the amount of time that a property has to have been empty before a grant will be offered and some will only offer grants if the property is to be made available for private letting through a Registered Social Landlord. More information about buying empty houses can be obtained from the Empty Homes Agency (www.emptyhomes.com).

- **Loan Scheme for Housing Repairs:** some local authorities will offer loans to homeowners and landlords who are wishing to repair and renovate their property. The loans are interest free and repayable by homeowners either when the property is sold or bequeathed, or, in the case of landlords, after five years. You should check that this is the most suitable method of raising finances, as, in the event of your death, your children will need to pay back the loan, whether or not they sell the property. Contact your local authority for more information about this grant.

Schemes and eligibility criteria vary throughout the UK, so you should contact your local authority direct for information about the grants and loans that are available in your area. Also, you should note that most local authorities will not offer a loan or grant if the work has already been carried out and most will need to approve the contractors that you have chosen before the work commences.

Protecting your finances

It is essential that you protect your finances and your investment. The best way to protect your property is to make sure that you have a good insurance policy in place (see chapter 10) and this is also the case with your finances. Today there are many different policies available and it is important that you do not try to cut costs and neglect this type of insurance, although you should shop around for the best deal. The types of insurance you should consider to protect your finances for you and your family include mortgage payment protection insurance, critical illness cover and life insurance. More information about this type of cover and other insurance policies that you should consider to help to protect your property investment is provided in chapter 10.

Summary

You must make sure that you are in a secure financial position before you make your property investment, and that you have a contingency fund available to cover for problems that may occur with your property. It is important to produce a profit/loss plan and a cash flow forecast, especially if you hope to raise finance through external backers or set up a property business. If you are hoping to take out a mortgage, obtain a grant or raise money through setting up a partnership, you must make sure that your children are not saddled with your debts if you should die unexpectedly. This can be done by ensuring that you take out adequate insurance and through planning your finances and estate carefully.

Once you have carried out a careful assessment of your finances, you need to think about the type of property investment in which you wish to become involved. This will depend on your personal and family circumstances, your preferences and those of your child, the age of your child and the type of investment in which it is prudent and viable to become involved. The next chapter offers advice for parents who are thinking about helping their child onto the property ladder.

Part 2:
Choosing how to invest

CHAPTER 7
Helping your child onto the property ladder

The rapid rise in house prices in the UK has meant that it is becoming harder for first-time buyers to step onto the property ladder. Parents are now finding that children have to live at home, or rent accommodation, for longer periods of time, until they are able to save enough money for a deposit and earn enough to meet monthly mortgage payments.

If you would like to help your child onto the property ladder, there are a number of ways that you can do this. For example, you could give him the money to pay a deposit on a property, which would help to reduce the size of loan he would need. Or you could take out a joint mortgage with your child, becoming co-owners of the property and increasing his borrowing power. Alternatively, you could decide to act as a guarantor on the mortgage, which would mean that the house would be owned by your child, but that the mortgage would be calculated on your income, again, increasing his borrowing power.

If you decide to help your child onto the property ladder in any of the ways described above, it is important to be aware of the advantages and disadvantages, understand the financial implications, know about the legal issues and understand the tax implications of your decisions, for you and your child. These issues are discussed in this chapter.

Assessing the advantages and disadvantages

In Table 1 the advantages and disadvantages of investing in property were outlined (see chapter 1). If you are thinking about investing in property by helping your child onto the property ladder, there are other advantages and disadvantages which you should be aware of before you make your investment. These are outlined in Table 4 below.

TABLE 4: THE ADVANTAGES AND DISADVANTAGES OF HELPING YOUR CHILD ONTO THE PROPERTY LADDER

ADVANTAGES	DISADVANTAGES
You are able to help your child onto the property ladder when he may not be able to afford to do so himself.	Your child may become financially dependent on you and less able or willing to fend for himself financially.
Your child will have his own home and will learn to become more independent, dealing with issues necessary for home ownership and independent living.	As you have helped him financially and you may have a stake in the property, you may be tempted to interfere too much in his independent life. Your child may resent you for too much interference. This can lead to arguments and a breakdown in family relationships.
You will be able to reclaim your own home.	You may miss your children and they may miss you.
If you buy wisely, you could make a good return on your investment.	If you do not buy wisely, you could lose your money and your child may be unable to sell his home when he wishes due to negative equity or no interest from potential purchasers. Your cash is tied up in the property and cannot be accessed in emergencies.

It may please you to give money to your child which can be put to good use in property and not wasted on other things.

Your child may have to pay IHT if you die within seven years of making the gift and if it is over your annual exemption. There may also be CGT and SDLT implications on your gift for you and/or your child.

Your child has a safe and secure home and you can help him to meet monthly mortgage payments.

A change in circumstances may mean that you or your child cannot meet the monthly mortgage payments. If you are joint owners, you are both liable for the whole loan. Your child may face the possibility of repossession and eviction if there is no adequate insurance protection. You may both end up with a bad credit history and have problems obtaining a mortgage in the future.

You have a stake in the property and a say in what your child should do in it. You see your stake in the property as a long-term investment.

Your child may have very different ideas about what he would like to do in his own home. He may not want you interfering in his life and may see your help as short term only. He may want to buy you out as soon as possible and you may not want this to happen.

You are able to take advantage of a short-term investment opportunity to help your child onto the property ladder until he can repay you and fend for himself.

Your child is unable to repay your loan, or lacks the motivation to repay once he is settled. You are unable to get your money back and family relationships suffer as a result.

You can invest in property in a more tax efficient way by buying the property in your child's name. There will be no CGT to pay when your child sells the property if it is his main home. There will be

SDLT will need to be paid by your child if the property is in his name. If you help him with this payment by making a gift, there could be IHT implications if you die within seven years of making the gift (see chapter 4).

no IHT liability on your
death as the property is
in your child's name.

As you can see from this table, the advantages and disadvantages in this type of investment depend on your family circumstances, your finances and those of your child, the type of property, the type of financial help you are willing to provide and the type of investment that you and your child envisage. If you want to avoid problems, it is imperative that you have a full and frank discussion with your child so that you are both clear about what you hope to gain from the investment. It is important to seek professional advice, especially when there may be tax implications, and you should draw up a legal document between you and your child that makes your respective responsibilities and expectations clear (see below).

Understanding the financial implications

There are a number of financial implications that you should be aware of, and these depend on the way in which you would like to help your child onto the property ladder:

- If you intend to take out a joint mortgage with your child, you must be in a secure financial position to do so. Also, you need to be sure that your child can meet his share of the mortgage each month. This is because both you and your child are jointly liable for repaying the whole loan. Also, there may be SDLT implications if your child hopes to buy your share at a later stage, depending on the value of his share of the property (see below).

- If you decide to act as a guarantor, your child is able to borrow more money than he could if the mortgage was assessed on his income. Therefore, you must make sure that your child is not overstretched financially. It could be tempting for him to buy a more expensive property, and then struggle to meet mortgage payments each month. As the guarantor you will be liable for all, or a portion of, the mortgage, so you must make sure that you have the finances in place if your child should default on the loan (see below).

- In cases where you intend to give money to your child to help him put down a deposit on a house, you must make it clear whether the money is a gift or a loan. Also, you must be aware of the IHT implications of this type of gift and make sure that you make use of annual exemptions, relief and transfers (see chapters 3 and 4).

- If you have the money available, you may choose to buy a house outright for your child. However, if you decide to do this, you must have other funds available that you can use in emergencies. If you tie up all your capital in a property investment, your child would lose his home if you needed to sell and you would be at the mercy of short-term fluctuations in the housing market if you had to sell at the wrong time.

If you choose to take out a mortgage with your child, becoming either a co-owner or a guarantor, you should consider worst case scenarios and make sure that you are protected financially should problems arise. For example, while your child is single and living on his own you may trust him to make monthly payments on time, and to protect your investment; however, what would happen if he met someone who was less scrupulous, who was able to move into his property and persuade him to act in a way that may be against your wishes?

Equity release

Some parents do not have enough savings to help their children onto the property ladder, but instead choose to remortgage or take out an equity release plan on their own home to free equity from the value of their house. The different types of equity release products include:

- A home reversion plan where a company buys a share of the home. When the property is sold the company takes its share from the proceeds. The recent rapid increase in house prices has meant that the amount owed to the company can be substantial. This has led to problems with people who have inherited a property being forced out of their home to repay the share of a plan taken out by their deceased parents.

- A home income plan where a lender gives you a mortgage that you use to buy a lifetime income or annuity. Interest payments are taken from this income and the loan is paid off when the property is sold.

- An interest-only mortgage where a lump sum is loaned against the value of the property. Interest on the mortgage is repaid monthly and the final loan repaid when the house is sold. With this type of agreement you must make sure that you have money invested elsewhere on which you can draw if the value of the property drops and you cannot pay off the loan.

- A lifetime mortgage where a sum of money is borrowed, either as a lump sum or on a monthly basis (i.e. an agreed monthly sum is released to you, as the borrower). With this type of mortgage there are no monthly repayments to make as the interest is added to the loan and the whole amount is repaid when you die or move into long-term care, usually from the sale of the house.

If you choose to release equity on your home, again, you must make sure that you are in a secure financial position to do so safely without jeopardising your own financial security, and that of your children when they come to inherit your property. Recently, there has been a great deal of media coverage about scandalous equity release plans that have forced homeowners from their property. Indeed, the consumer group Which? describes equity release policies as 'expensive, inflexible and risky'. If you are thinking about following this route, you must seek professional advice and make sure that you use a reputable organisation. Use the firm checker on the FSA website to check whether a firm is regulated and able to offer advice about equity release products (www.fsa.gov.uk/register). More information about equity release is provided in chapter 9.

Low incomes

If you want to help your child onto the property ladder because he is on a low income, you should first check whether he is eligible for financial help through various government schemes. In some cases it may be more sensible, financially, for your child to receive help through these schemes rather than receive financial help from you.

If your child is a key public sector worker such as a nurse or a teacher, he may be eligible to receive help with buying his home through the Key Worker Living Programme. To be eligible for this scheme your child must be intending to buy a property in London or the South East or East of England. For more information about this scheme and other house buying schemes that are available for people on low incomes, visit the Communities and Local Government website (www.communities. gov.uk/housing). If your child works for the NHS, he should visit the Housing for NHS Staff website, which provides more information about help available for members of staff who wish to buy a home (www.housing.nhs.uk).

Adult children who are on a low income may be eligible for additional financial help through the tax credit system. More information about tax issues and tax credits for people on low incomes can be obtained from the Low Incomes Tax Reform Group (www.litrg.org.uk).

Author's note

I have a friend who is a teacher, living in Brighton. She could not afford to buy her own home so her parents offered to help by paying the deposit. However, my friend still did not earn enough to get the mortgage she required and her parents were unable to act as guarantors or take out a joint mortgage because they were retired and only received a state pension. My friend sought advice from her local CAB, who told her about the Key Worker Living Programme. She received a loan to help her to buy a flat and is now happily settled in her new home.

Providing financial help

There are two main ways that parents can help their children get on the property ladder. The first is by providing a lump sum to pay for upfront costs such as SDLT, a deposit or solicitor's fees. The second is to help them obtain a mortgage, by acting as a guarantor or helping with monthly payments.

Giving money to your child

If you decide to give money to your child, you are able to make a gift of £3,000 a year without IHT implications. Remember that both parents can make this gift, which means that you can give £6,000 to your child per year. This figure could rise to £12,000 if both parents have not made use of their annual exemption for the previous year. This could be enough to pay legal fees, SDLT and part of the deposit, which may be all your child needs to help him onto the property ladder.

Indeed, if you could afford to do so, both parents could gift a total of £120,000 over 20 years (£3,000 each, per year) that is exempt from IHT, at today's rates. Your child could deposit these annual gifts in a high interest savings account until he has enough capital to begin looking for a suitable property, which he is then able to buy in his name. This will reduce your children's IHT bill on your death and help them buy somewhere to live while you are alive. Alternatively, you could choose to give them more than the annual exempt amount of £3,000 in one year, but you will need to survive the gift by seven years for it to be exempt from IHT (see chapter 4). Examples of other action that you could take, depending on your circumstances, are provided at the end of this book.

Loaning money to your child

Some parents decide to provide money for their child by making a loan, rather than a gift, to help him buy a house. If this is the case, you should make sure that you have a written agreement about the terms of the loan and that your child is clear about the terms, conditions and repayment period. You also need to decide whether you are intending to take an equity stake in the property in return for your contribution. If this is the case, again, you will need a written agreement (see below). Some mortgage companies will be concerned about your having a stake in the property and will want to see your agreement, or a letter outlining the terms of the agreement.

If you have specified that your child should pay back the loan by a specific date, the mortgage company will want to know how much the repayments are likely to be and will take this into account when assessing how much your child can borrow from it. This will be the case whether or not you have decided to take an equity stake in the property. Also, mortgage companies are likely to request more comprehensive details about the type of loan agreement that you have with your child as the credit crunch begins to bite.

Helping with the mortgage

There are several ways in which you can help your child with his mortgage. These include taking out a joint mortgage, a guarantor mortgage, a first-start mortgage or a family offset mortgage as described below. Eligibility criteria, including maximum ages for parents and minimum ages for children, apply, so obtain information about specific schemes from your financial adviser or chosen lender. Also, you should note that the type of ownership of the property, in particular whether it is owned by you, your child, or jointly, has implications for IHT, CGT and SDLT. These tax implications are discussed below.

Joint mortgages

You may decide that you want to help your child by making contributions towards his mortgage repayments. However, these contributions will not be taken into account when a lender decides whether your child should be approved for a mortgage unless you are named on the mortgage. If your child is unable to secure a mortgage on his own income, you will need to think about taking out a joint mortgage, which means that both you and your child will be named on the mortgage deed and that your combined income will be taken into account when the amount of loan is determined. If you already have a mortgage, your borrowing power may be reduced.

To be able to raise a mortgage on a property you actually need to own it, or at least part of it, so this type of agreement means that you become joint owners and that you are both named on the title deeds. As we saw in chapter 2, there are two main types of joint ownership – joint tenants or tenants in common. In general, it is better that parents and children become tenants in common, as it means that each party can sell his share while he is still alive, or dispose of his share through his Will when he dies. Indeed, some lenders will insist on this type of ownership. You will need a legal agreement that sets out what will happen if either party wishes to sell his share during his lifetime (see below). This should specify that a professional valuation will be undertaken, that the share will be offered to the co-owner (you or your child) and that the property will be sold if the co-owner does not want, or cannot afford, to buy the other share. However, all circumstances are different, so you should seek professional advice tailored to your needs.

When you take out a joint mortgage you do so on the basis of 'joint and several liability', which means that both you and your child are liable for repaying the whole loan. If you decide on this option, you will need to make sure that your child can repay his share of the loan on a monthly basis, and work out how the repayments can be made if your child is unable to meet the payments. Also, you will need to decide what will happen if changing circumstances mean that you are unable to meet repayments. Taking out mortgage payment protection insurance is important to protect both you and your child and to protect your property from repossession (see chapter 10).

This type of arrangement may have SDLT implications for your child if he decides to buy your share of the property at a later date (see chapter 5). Also, your child's home will be considered as your second property. This means that you could be subject to CGT when it comes to giving up the property, whether you sell your share to your child or you both decide to sell the property. If you are tenants in common and you should die unexpectedly, your share will be added to your estate for IHT purposes, but any outstanding mortgage debt on the property can be deducted from the total value of your estate (see chapter 3). If you are joint tenants, however, your share of the property automatically passes to your child if you die and will not be added to your estate for IHT purposes (see chapter 2). However, your child will be liable to pay any outstanding mortgage debt on the property so you should take out adequate life insurance to cover the mortgage in the event of your death (see chapter 10).

Joint mortgages between your children

Another option is that your children take out a joint mortgage between them as they could add their savings together to pay the deposit and their joint income would be taken into account when their borrowing limit is assessed. This tends to be three and a half or four times their combined income. If your children are interested in this option, they should be encouraged to rent a property together first so that they can see whether they are able to live together away from the parental home. Again, all children would be legally liable to meet the mortgage repayments and if they experience difficulties all of them could have problems with bad credit history.

With any type of joint mortgage, you should draw up a legal agreement (sometimes called a 'Property Co-ownership Agreement' or 'Trust Deed') stating the amount that each person has contributed towards the deposit and repayments, and what will happen if the agreement ended. This agreement should help to prevent misunderstandings and disagreements and should try to cover most eventualities. You will need to instruct your solicitor to draw up this agreement to ensure that all the paperwork is in order and that the agreement is legally binding.

Guarantor mortgages

Another way to help your child onto the property ladder is to act as a guarantor when he takes out a mortgage. This type of mortgage is used when a parent decides to guarantee the whole amount of the mortgage because his child is on a low income, or when he decides to guarantee a part of the mortgage to help his child to meet a mortgage shortfall. For example, if your child earns £20,000 per annum he could borrow around £80,000, depending on the lender policy. If the property he wants to purchase is worth £130,000, there is a shortfall of £50,000. As a parent you can offer a guarantee to cover this shortfall so that your child can obtain the size loan he requires.

Under this arrangement your child is the owner of the property and is the only person to be named on the mortgage, but the amount that he can borrow is based on your financial circumstances rather than his. When a lender assesses your suitability for a guarantor mortgage it will want to know about the level of your income and your financial commitments, such as other mortgages and loans. It is not necessary for you to be employed to take out this type of mortgage – the lender will assess your overall financial circumstances when deciding whether you can act as a guarantor.

With this type of agreement the lender requires you, as the guarantor, to be liable for all, or a portion of, the mortgage and if your child defaults you will have to find the money to repay the loan. Therefore, this type of mortgage may be a better option for parents who are mortgage-free, settled in their own home and who have no intention of moving as it can be a considerable financial commitment if your child is unable to meet his monthly repayments. Also, this type of mortgage may influence your ability to obtain a mortgage for yourself in the future.

As the amount of loan is based on your financial circumstances rather than that of your child you will have to make sure that your child is not tempted to take out too large a mortgage. Also, this type of arrangement may require a larger deposit than other types of mortgage, so you or your child will need to have enough savings to meet this deposit.

Once your child's income has increased enough so that he can support the loan it is possible for you to be released from the mortgage and your responsibilities as guarantor, usually free of charge. You should note, however, that with this type of agreement you are not in the communication loop as you are not named on the mortgage deeds. This means that you may not know about potential problems until the lender contacts you to bring the guarantee into action.

There are no IHT or CGT implications with the type of ownership as your child owns the property so it will not be added to your estate when you die, and it is his principal private residence so there will be no CGT when he sells the property at a later date (see chapters 3 and 5).

First-start mortgages

This type of mortgage is offered by some lenders and has an advantage over other types of joint mortgage in that it is possible for parents to agree to let their child become the sole owner of the property, although you can choose to be joint owners if you wish. Having your child as the sole owner may save problems arising at a later date with SDLT, CGT and IHT. However, you are still jointly liable for mortgage repayments and for the total loan. Also, you should seek professional advice and draw up a legal agreement if you are thinking about enabling your child to become the sole owner of a property in which you have invested considerable amounts of money.

With this type of mortgage your income, after commitments, is added to the income of your child when the amount of mortgage is assessed, thus increasing his borrowing power. Again, you should make sure that your child is not tempted to take on too large a loan, and all reputable lenders will make sure that this is clear before they agree to lend money.

Unlike guarantor mortgages, to obtain this type of mortgage you will need to be under the age of 60 and in employment. If your child intends to borrow more than 95 per cent of the purchase price, you will need to own your own home outright or have had a mortgage on the property for at least three years.

Family offset mortgages

As a parent you may be concerned that, if you give your savings to your child as a deposit or by making mortgage repayments, you may lose your money or not have access to your funds in a financial emergency. In these cases you may find that a family offset mortgage is more appropriate. Under this arrangement your child takes out a mortgage in his name and you deposit your savings with the same lender under your name. The mortgage is offset against your savings, which means that the interest on your child's mortgage is charged on the balance, rather than the whole amount, thus reducing your child's monthly payments. Although you will not receive interest on your savings, the money is safe if you need it at a later date. Also, you can withdraw money when you need to, although this will increase your child's interest payments.

With this type of arrangement you have more control over your money because you can access it at any time and it is not tied up in the property. However, in most cases, the lender will insist that your name goes on the mortgage deed, making you jointly liable for repayments, which may not be what you want. Also, there will be no CGT to pay when your child sells the property, if he has made it his home, and there will be no IHT liability for your child when you die, because the property is in his name.

Taking out an equity stake

Parents who are hoping to make a profit from their investment, in addition to helping their child onto the property ladder, may wish to take an equity stake in the property. With this type of arrangement you make an agreement with your child that in return for the capital you have invested you will own a percentage of the property. For example, you may decide to pay a lump sum for the deposit, but your child has full responsibility for paying the mortgage. Rather than regard the money as a loan, you regard it as an investment and you would like to see a return on this investment in the future. You can choose to take an equity stake over a fixed period of time or until your child sells the property. At the end of the term you get back your initial investment plus your share of the appreciation. However, you should note that some mortgage providers will let you take out an equity stake, whereas others will not, so you will need to obtain comprehensive information and advice from your chosen lender. If you choose to take an equity stake, you should obtain the services of a solicitor who specialises in property law who can draw up a suitable agreement for you.

Some parents feel that taking out an equity stake helps to protect their money and gives them more control over what their child does with the property. However, some children see this as unnecessary interference and may come to resent their parents' involvement in the long run. Your children must stand on their own two feet at some point in their lives, and if you take an equity stake in their property it may be prudent not to make this a permanent arrangement, but instead have a release clause that can be put into action when your child is financially secure. Details of this should be included in your agreement (see below). Also, you should note that there may be IHT and CGT implications, depending on the size of your stake in the property. If you are hoping to make a long-term investment in property for your children, there are other options available, such as buy-to-let or buying a second home, which may be more appropriate for your needs (see chapters 8 and 9).

Drawing up an agreement

If you decide to help your child onto the property ladder, it is essential that you draw up a legal and binding agreement that covers all eventualities. This is the case when providing a loan to your child or helping with any of the types of mortgage described above. This will help to protect you, your child and your money against unforeseen and unplanned problems that could arise, or misunderstandings and disagreements that could occur in the future. Also, some lenders will insist that you have such an agreement before offering a mortgage. Although agreements will vary depending on individual and family circumstances, you should think about the inclusion of the following points:

- your name, address and telephone number;

- the name of your child;

- the address of the property that is to be purchased;

- details of the mortgage offer;

- exact details and terms of the agreement;

- how the agreement can be terminated;

- amount of loan, how and by what date it is to be repaid (if relevant);

- the proportion of the mortgage repayments to be paid by each party (if relevant);

- size of equity stake held by parent, and length of time over which it is to be held (if relevant);

- the share of equity to which each owner is entitled on sale (if relevant);

- the type of insurance to be taken out;

- who is responsible for making payments and what will happen if one party ceases to pay;

- what will happen upon death of either party;

- relevant signatures;

- name, address and signature of a witness.

When drawing up this type of agreement you should seek specialist advice. To find a solicitor that specialises in these issues in your area, visit the Law Society website (www.lawsociety.org.uk).

Understanding tax implications

If you decide to help your child onto the property ladder, you must be aware of the tax implications, both for you and for your child. Any gift that you make to your child over the exempt amount is liable to IHT if you do not survive for seven years after having made the gift, so you need to make sure that your child understands this and would be able to meet any IHT bill that may be due (see chapters 3 and 4). The type of ownership of the property also has IHT implications. If you are a sole or joint owner, your share of the property will be added to your estate for IHT purposes, although mortgage debt can be deducted from the total.

In cases where you have an equity stake in the property and you hope that your child will be able to buy your stake from you at a later date, he may have to pay SDLT, if your stake is over the current SDLT levels at the time he makes the purchase from you (see chapter 5). Again, the value of your stake in the property will be added to your estate for IHT purposes.

If you are joint owners of a property and your child decides to sell at a later date, he would not have to pay CGT if the property is his main residence, but you may be liable to pay CGT on the profit that has been made on your share of the property, as it is not your main residence. For more information about tax implications see chapters 3 and 5.

Summary

Many parents are thinking about helping their children onto the property ladder as, due to rising house prices, it has become increasingly difficult for first-time buyers to buy a property. There are several ways that parents can choose to do this, such as providing gifts or loans for deposits and helping with mortgages by acting as a guarantor or taking out a joint mortgage. All agreements (unless you have made a gift outright) should be legally binding and produced with the advice and guidance of a solicitor, as this will help to protect your investment and your child's home. Also, it is important that you discuss your plans thoroughly with your child so that everyone is clear about what you are trying to do with your investment.

If your child is hoping to go away to college or university you may be thinking about investing in property by buying him a house in which to live while he is studying. This can prove to be a good investment if you buy wisely and if your child intends to study in a location where house prices are rising. These issues are discussed in the following chapter.

CHAPTER 8

Buying property for your student child

In 2006 the Direct Line UK Second Property Index was launched to conduct research into the amount and type of second properties held in the UK (see chapter 9). The research found that there are currently 327,000 'handout homes' in the UK. A quarter of these (83,000) were purchased by parents to house their student children at university, which is a 26 per cent increase since 2000. The Index anticipates that student occupied second homes will reach the 100,000 mark by 2010. If your child is going away to college or university, then parents buying a house for him to live in while he is there is becoming an increasingly popular and useful way to invest in property.

However, there are many issues which you should be aware of, for example, understanding the rules and responsibilities associated with becoming a landlord and letting property. Also, you need to be aware of the financial implications for you and your child and how to choose the right property and make sure that you do not lose money. These issues are discussed in this chapter. There is also a helpful book by Lynette Tomlinson called *How to Make Money from Student Property* (Lawpack, 2008).

Assessing the advantages and disadvantages

If you are thinking about buying a property for your student child, it is important to think about the advantages and disadvantages of this type of investment (see Table 5). As with other types of property investment, this will depend on your family circumstances and available finances, and it will also depend on where your child decides to study; for example, if your child chooses a university far away from you and you intend to become a landlord, you need to consider the cost, time and practicalities involved in visiting your property (see case study 4, below). It is possible to pass over the management of your property to a letting agent or property management company, but you will need to work out whether this is a prudent move to make, financially (see below).

TABLE 5: THE ADVANTAGES AND DISADVANTAGES OF BUYING PROPERTY FOR YOUR STUDENT CHILD

ADVANTAGES	DISADVANTAGES
The buy-to-let market is still doing well in some popular student areas, with competitive mortgages on the market and substantial profits to be made with wise investment. Although the credit crunch has reduced the number of buy-to-let mortgages available, it is still possible to find some competitive deals if you can pay a large deposit and convince the lender that there are tenants available. Also, due to the credit crunch, some buy-to-let investors are selling, which means that, in some areas, students	If you choose the wrong mortgage for your personal circumstances and make a bad property choice, you could lose out substantially. Taking out a buy-to-let mortgage in your name will influence your chance of obtaining another mortgage at a later date. There are other mortgages available that may be more suitable (see chapter 7). If the buy-to-let market is saturated in the place where your child is studying, you may struggle to get tenants for your property. Also, you may struggle to find tenants during the long holidays when students return to their homes.

are competing for fewer properties and are having to pay higher rents. This is certainly the case in the town in which our property company is located.

It gives you peace of mind to know that your child has somewhere safe and secure to live while he is studying and that he is not at the mercy of unscrupulous landlords.	You, or your child, will need to adopt the role of landlord if you intend to let any other rooms in the property. There are rules and regulations involved with this and the role does not suit everybody (see case study 4, below).
You can let other rooms in the property to your child's friends and thus increase the rental income from your property.	It is hard to take your child's friends to court for rent arrears or damage to your property. You, or your child, may find it hard to chase late payments. You can avoid some problems by making sure that your tenants sign a tenancy agreement (see below).
House prices are rising faster in major university towns than in other areas of the UK. With wise choices you can make a considerable profit if you decide to sell when your child finishes his course.	Your child will need to study in an area where house prices are still rising and this may not match his learning choices. He may not want to leave his home when his course finishes and this could cause friction. There could be CGT to pay when you sell if the property is in your name (see chapter 5).
This is a useful way to provide financial support for your child when the costs of education are soaring, especially with the introduction of variable tuition fees. Your child will not have to worry about meeting rent payments each	Your money will be tied up in the property and if you need to sell quickly to raise cash it will be very disruptive for your child's studies. If you have let other rooms in the house, it will be difficult to sell the property while it is tenanted.

month, if you have decided not to charge him rent.	
You can choose where your child lives and can have control over what he does in the property.	Your child may have different ideas about where he wants to live and what he does in the property, which may cause tension and friction.
Your children can live together and keep each other company while they are studying.	Siblings may not want to study in the same place. If you have already bought a property in a specific location, this will severely restrict their learning choices. Your children may lack interest and motivation and may not succeed on their course if it is not something they have chosen. Siblings may not live well together away from the family home.
You can test the water to find out whether you have what it takes to enter the buy-to-let market and can consider buying other properties for investment purposes if it works well.	You may find it difficult to get tenants for your property. You may encounter too many problems with damage and arrears. Tenants expect a lot and you are not willing to be on call 24 hours a day. You may find that becoming a landlord does not suit you, personally.

As you can see from Table 5, the advantages and disadvantages of this type of investment depend on what sort of accommodation you intend to buy, the type of mortgage, the place where your child wishes to study and whether you or your child is willing to become a landlord. To make a successful investment and to avoid family arguments you will need to discuss these issues with your child so that you all fully understand what you are trying to do and what you hope to gain from the investment.

Understanding the financial implications

When you consider the financial implications of your investment decisions, you need to think about the costs of sending your child to college and university, the cost of the different types of accommodation and the tax implications of your investment choices.

Tuition and maintenance costs

Higher education is becoming increasingly expensive, with students having to pay variable fees of up to £3,145 in England, Wales and Northern Ireland (2008/09 levels). Welsh students who decide to study in Wales can receive a fee grant of £1,890 to help with the cost of tuition fees, but students in England and Northern Ireland will need to pay the fees themselves. Universities offer grants, bursaries and scholarships to help some students meet payments, but as entitlement to most of these is assessed on parental income, your child may not be entitled to any financial help. Also, students can take out a fee loan to cover tuition fees and this is paid back in the same way as the loan for maintenance (see below). Currently, Scottish students do not have to pay variable fees if they study at a Scottish university.

While at college or university your child will also need to meet maintenance costs, which includes accommodation. There is a government higher education maintenance grant available, but again, the full grant is only available for students with a household income of less than £25,000. A partial grant is available above this amount, but if your household income is above £60,005 your child will not be entitled to any grant at all (2008/09 levels). Some universities offer subsidised accommodation, or accommodation vouchers, but again these are only available for students from low income families.

Student loans

Student loans are available to help with tuition fees and maintenance and your child will start to pay back the loan when he is earning £15,000 or more after he has finished his studies. Many parents feel that their child should take advantage of the student loan as this is cheaper than those offered by commercial banks, building societies and other lenders. Indeed, some children have been encouraged to take out a loan to use as a deposit on a house, which is then sold after university. As house prices have been growing at a quicker rate than interest on the loan, this has provided financial gain for students and parents. More information about student loans and grants can be obtained from Student Finance Direct (www.studentsupportdirect.co.uk).

University accommodation costs

As someone who is interested in investing in property, you may have decided that you are going to buy a property in which your child can live before his university course begins. However, you should note that most universities and the National Union of Students (NUS) recommend that first-year students live in halls of residence so that they can acclimatise and have the chance to mix with other students before they find accommodation elsewhere in the second year.

If your child lives in halls in the first year, the price of university accommodation depends on the type of rooms available and whether you choose catered or self-catering halls. Most universities now have a selection of accommodation to suit all tastes and budgets, and many institutions give first choice and priority to first-year students. Perhaps surprisingly, accommodation costs do not vary a great deal between geographical locations. Instead, they vary between types of accommodation and the facilities available. To give you an idea of how much you can expect to pay for different types of university accommodation in the South of England and the Midlands, see Tables 6 and 7. All prices are based on 2008/09 levels.

TABLE 6: UNIVERSITY ACCOMMODATION IN THE SOUTH OF ENGLAND

	University-owned house	Large halls of residence off campus	Purpose built halls on campus
Number of rooms	8	188	298
Weekly rent	£71	£65–£69	£94–£147
Internet access	No	No	Yes
En suite	No	No	Yes
Catered	No	No	Choice available, reflected in price

TABLE 7: UNIVERSITY ACCOMMODATION IN THE MIDLANDS

	Individual student flats	Large halls of residence off campus	Small halls of residence on campus
Number of rooms	165	321	50
Weekly rent	£78.70	£70–£135	£62
Internet access	Unspecified	No	No
En suite	No	Some en suite	No
Catered	No	Choice available, reflected in price	No

As you can see from Tables 6 and 7, in most cases the more expensive accommodation tends to be catered, en suite with Internet access available in each room. The more your child pays, the more facilities he tends to receive. In general, rent covers heating, lighting and water. Most universities ask that fees are paid in three instalments at the beginning of each term, preferably by direct debit.

Private rented accommodation costs

If you decide to buy a property that you are going to let to other students, you should note that private accommodation rents vary considerably over the country and within specific areas of towns and cities. Most towns and cities have areas within them that are popular with students. In general, these tend to be areas of terraced houses that can provide rooms for four or five students in each property, located within walking distance of the college or university. Students usually have to pay the following weekly rent for this type of property:

- London £85–£125

- Leeds £55–£68

- Newcastle £42–£55

- Southampton £60–£87

Contact your child's university accommodation office for more information about prices specific to their location (see below). This will help you to plan your finances and work out the profit that could be made on your investment (see chapter 6).

The Tenancy Deposit Protection Scheme

If you choose to become a landlord, you should ask for a deposit to protect you against any damage that might occur to your property. A new Tenancy Deposit Protection Scheme has been introduced by the government in an attempt to protect deposits from being withheld unfairly by landlords. The government has awarded the contract to three companies and you can find out about each scheme by visiting the relevant websites (www.thedisputeservice.co.uk, www.depositprotection.com, www.my deposits.co.uk). Deposits usually range from £250 to £350 or are equivalent to the rent for one month. They should be paid before your tenants move in and you will need to provide them with details of the deposit scheme that is to be used within 14 days of the start of the tenancy agreement.

There are two types of scheme available:

1   a custodial scheme in which the money is held by the scheme until the end of the tenancy; and

2   an insurance-based scheme in which the landlord keeps the deposit, but pays a premium to the insurer.

You will need to decide which scheme is more appropriate for your needs; for example, some landlords need the money from the deposit to repair and maintain the property during the tenancy. In this case an insurance-based scheme would be more appropriate. More information about the different types of scheme can be obtained from the government's information website (www.direct.gov.uk).

Income Tax

As we saw in the previous chapter, it may be more tax efficient to buy the property in your child's name, especially if you hope to save on CGT and IHT. If the property is in your child's name and he decides to let rooms in his home, he could claim Rent-a-Room Relief, which means that the first

£4,250 (equivalent to £81.73 per week) rent per tax year is exempt from Income Tax. Your child must also be living in the property to take advantage of this relief. This relief is available to individuals who let furnished rooms in their only or main home.

If your child chooses to take advantage of this scheme, he can't claim any expenses relating to the letting (e.g. wear and tear, insurance, repairs, heating and lighting). This is because these expense claims are only available to landlords who have an income from rents of at least £2,500 per year who declare all of their letting income, pay Income Tax on the rent and claim expenses on their tax return (see chapter 5). In general, these are landlords who do not live in the property, or people who are letting several units within a dwelling. If you wish to own the property in your name and take on the responsibilities of being a landlord, you may be able to claim these expenses yourself. Your child will not need to declare his income, or keep records of his expenses while his rental income remains under £4,250, because the Rent-a-Room Relief is provided automatically.

If your child intends to take in lodgers he will need to check with his lender that it is permissible. For more information about mortgages see chapter 7. For more information about the Rent-a-Room scheme visit www.direct.gov.uk.

Some parents, however, decide that they would like to buy the property in their name and take on the landlord responsibilities. This may be because you do not trust your child to be responsible enough, or you may not wish to burden your child with extra responsibilities while he is studying. As a landlord letting rooms to students, you will have to pay tax on any profit you make from letting your property if your total net income, including this profit, is more than your Income Tax allowance for the year. It is possible to offset any expenses such as fuel, insurance and maintenance costs against your rental income, if they are incurred when you let the property (see chapter 5).

Finding suitable properties

If your child decides to live in halls of residence for his first year he will be able to get to know the location and will know the more popular student areas and the safer areas in which to live. Also, he will have made some friends in the first year and will know with whom he would like to live in the second year. This will make it easier for you to choose a property to buy and to find tenants, if you have decided to let rooms in the property. Also, it will give you plenty of time to buy a house before your child starts his second year (see case study 4, below). However, if you decide to delay purchasing the property for a year your child will have to pay rent in the first year and the profit that you make on your investment could be reduced. Discuss the issue with your child to help you to decide upon the most appropriate course of action.

Researching unfamiliar locations

In cases where your child is moving to an unfamiliar location to study and you wish to buy in his first year you must carry out comprehensive research into the location and conduct a thorough price analysis before you buy a property. If you are hoping to make money on your investment, you must buy the right property, at the right price in the right location. Checklists to help you choose a suitable property are provided in Appendices 2 and 3. Also, you will need to make sure that you allow plenty of time for the house purchase to complete before the start of term (see case study 4, below).

The property market in some areas of the UK is not performing as well as it is in other areas and, if your child chooses to study in one of these areas, you need to consider seriously whether it is the right time to buy a property. However, well-known university towns and cities, such as Bristol, Nottingham, Bath, Durham and Edinburgh, are still performing well and may provide a good investment opportunity if your child chooses a course in these areas. You can find out about average house prices and how these have changed in specific locations by using the regional house price map or postcode calculators on the Halifax website (visit www.hbosplc.com and click on Halifax UK House Price Index), the Nationwide website (visit www.nationwide.co.uk and click on Nationwide House Price Index) or Land Registry website (www.landregistry.gov.uk).

Choosing accommodation to let

If you are hoping to let your accommodation to other students, there are certain issues you should bear in mind when looking for suitable accommodation:

- Increasingly it is parents, rather than students, who choose accommodation. Therefore, choose a property that will appeal to parents and you will be more successful in letting your rooms. Parents want somewhere that looks safe and secure, in a decent neighbourhood, close to the college or university. They want a friendly, approachable landlord and want to know that other tenants will not cause problems for their children. Also, they want to see that the house is well equipped and nicely furnished. Gone are the days of dark and dingy student digs.

- Make sure that saturation point hasn't been reached. Some student areas are saturated with buy-to-let accommodation, offered by large property companies with which you would have to compete. If you buy in the second year, however, you can make sure that your child has already chosen tenants. Contact local letting agencies and the university accommodation office to find out whether there is still demand for student accommodation in the area.

- Some students are on a very tight budget, whereas other students receive a great deal of financial support, usually from their parents. You need to decide where you are going to position yourself in the market and make sure that this market is available in the area. Do you buy in a cheaper area and appeal to those on a budget, or do you buy in a more expensive area and appeal to those who have more money to spend? Which type is more likely to be successful? Accommodation officers, letting agents, management companies and lenders in the local area will be able to offer more advice.

Author's note

When we first started letting to students in 1996 it was individual students, or groups of students, who came to view the property. It was rare that they would bring parents with them. Now it is rare that a student will turn up without parents. Sometimes parents even come to view the accommodation on their own without their student child. Students used to ask questions such as 'where is the nearest pub?' or 'can my mates stay over?', whereas parents are much more interested in looking inside the oven or testing that the microwave and washer/dryer work. Fixtures, fittings and equipment have had to be replaced and updated to cater for parents who come to view.

University accommodation offices

All universities have a student accommodation office and your child should be encouraged to obtain an accommodation list as this will help you to research the more popular student locations and the amount of rent that can be charged. If you are hoping to let your property to other students, you can discuss this with the accommodation officer. He will offer advice about where to buy, the facilities you must provide and the rules and regulations to which you must adhere.

Most accommodation offices will provide a 'new landlord's pack' or enable you to join their private registration scheme. Universities will charge a small fee for this service and will want to see that you have the relevant gas and electricity safety certificates and that your accommodation complies with the local authority and university Code of Standards (see below).

Letting your accommodation

If you decide to let your property, you must draw up a tenancy agreement. Most student landlords use an Assured Shorthold Tenancy Agreement (see below). If you are a new landlord, it is best to obtain an existing agreement that you can use to avoid potential problems. The university accommodation officer or the Students' Union will be able to provide a copy of their preferred agreement and offer advice about letting student accommodation. The Residential Landlords Association (RLA) has produced a tenancy agreement which is free to members or available from their website for a one-off fee of £5 (www.rla.org.uk). If you are hoping to become a landlord as a long-term investment, you might find it useful to join the RLA or National Landlords Association (www.landlords.org.uk) as both organisations provide useful advice, information and support for landlords. You can also obtain a Furnished or Unfurnished Tenancy Agreement for England and Wales and a Lodger Agreement for England and Wales from Lawpack (www.lawpack.co.uk) for £9.99 each.

An Assured Shorthold Tenancy means that you can do the following:

- You can charge a market rent.

- You can get your property back after six months (subject to court orders).

- You may be able to evict your tenants if they cause annoyance to local people (subject to court orders).

- You can get your property back if your tenants owe more than two months' rent, provided the proper form of notice has been served (subject to court orders).

You should make sure that your tenancy agreement is clear and unambiguous and includes the following points:

- Your name, the name of your tenant and the address of the property.

- The date the tenancy is to begin.

- The duration of the tenancy.

- An accurate description of the property, including an inventory which should be agreed and signed separately. This should include information about responsibilities in terms of damage and breakages. You can use an independent inventory agent to undertake this task for you, if you are a first-time landlord (see www.theaiic.co.uk).

- The amount of rent payable, when and how often it should be paid and when it can be increased.

- The amount of deposit to be paid and details about the deposit scheme to be used.

- What you have included in the rent. You may choose to include utilities, but in general this is not a good idea as it encourages tenants to be more reckless with fuel than they might otherwise be. Some landlords decide to pay water charges, although, if you have a water meter it may be preferable that tenants pay.

- Information about the services you will provide as landlord. You have certain legal responsibilities, but you may wish to include other services, such as a cleaner once a week.

- Information about gaining access to the property and the amount of notice required.

- A detailed list of tenants' and landlord's responsibilities. You should include a clause that states that tenants must let you know when problems occur, as this will help you to maintain the property and show that you are a responsible landlord. Hopefully, your child will alert you to any problems but there may be occasions when your child is away or unable to do this for other reasons.

- Issues on which a tenant needs to seek your permission before acting. This could include carrying out improvements, subletting, having pets or smoking in the property.

- The length of notice you, or your tenants, must give if you or they require the tenancy to end.

If you have bought the property in your child's name and he decides to take in lodgers, different rules apply. More information can be obtained from the government booklet: *Letting Rooms in your Home: A guide for Resident Landlords*. The booklet can be downloaded from www.communities.gov.uk. Your child should be encouraged to read this booklet so that he understands his roles and responsibilities as landlord.

Knowing about student letting rules and regulations

Most universities work closely with the local authority to develop a Code of Standards, which must be met by all landlords who wish to register as student accommodation providers. This will lay out all the legal requirements for landlords and any additional standards deemed to be important by the local authority and the university. The legal requirements are as follows:

- It is the landlord's responsibility to maintain the property in good order, and to carry out any necessary repairs to the internal and external parts of the building and services. All structures, installations, services, sanitary fittings and heating systems must be maintained and kept in full working order.

- All gas appliances should be checked for safety every 12 months and this must be done by a CORGI-registered installer. You should request a Landlord's Gas Safety Certificate, a copy of which should be provided to your tenants. The cost of gas safety inspections depends on the type of inspection required and the type and number of appliances in the property, but should be in the region of £55–£100. More information about gas safety for landlords can be obtained from www.hse.gov.uk. Visit the CORGI website to find a registered installer in your area (www.trustcorgi.com).

- You must find out whether your property is a House in Multiple Occupation (HMO) and whether it will need to be licensed. An HMO is legally defined as any property that is occupied by persons who do not form a single household. Licensing criteria can vary between local authorities, but in general a licence will be needed if there are five or more people living in the property and the property has three or more storeys. More information about obtaining a licence can be obtained from your local authority or from www.communities.gov.uk.

- You are required to comply with the Furniture and Furnishings Fire Safety section of the Consumer Protection Act 1987 to ensure that all items of furniture are safe. Furniture which does not meet the required safety standard must be either replaced or treated with a flame retardant substance.

- You are required to comply with the Portable Appliance Safety section of the Consumer Protection Act 1987 to ensure that all electrical items are safe. All portable electrical appliances must be inspected and tested regularly by an approved electrician. The Consumer Protection Act makes it an offence for a landlord to provide any portable electrical appliance which is either electrically or physically unsafe and that would be a danger to tenants or visitors to the property. The cost of portable appliance testing varies, depending on the electrician that you use and the number of appliances that need testing, but should be in the range of £50 - £70 for up to ten appliances. You can find an approved contractor from the online databases of the National Inspection Council for Electrical Installation Contracting (NICEIC) (www.niceic.com), Electrical Safety Council (ESC) (www.electricalsafetycouncil.org.uk) or National Association of Professional Inspectors and Testers (NAPIT) (www.napit.org.uk).

- Your property must comply with the Housing Health and Safety Rating System (HHSRS). This is a new risk assessment tool used to assess potential risks to the health and safety of occupants in residential properties in England and Wales. Separate housing legislation applies to Northern Ireland and Scotland. In general, any property that comes to the attention of the local authority can be assessed and a charge will be made for the inspection. This is usually when a complaint has been made. To avoid this happening you should carry out an assessment of your property to determine whether there are any serious hazards that may cause a risk to your tenants. If so, you should make the necessary improvements as soon as possible. If you intend to register your property with the student accommodation office, someone will come to check that it meets the required standards. More information about the HHSRS can be obtained from www.communities.gov.uk.

All these conditions are legal requirements and must be met before you let your accommodation. Also, you should contact the university accommodation office to find out about its preferred standards when letting accommodation to its students. More information about student accommodation can be obtained from the NUS (www.nusonline.com).

Managing your property

You have to make decisions about who is going to manage your property. You could decide that you want to become a landlord and manage the property yourself. This option is cheaper than employing someone else, but you need to make sure that you live close enough to the property to make it feasible and that you understand and are able to fulfil this role (see case study 4, below).

Another cheap option is to buy a house in your child's name and have him take on the landlord responsibilities. If you choose this option, you have to make sure that your child understands his role and that he is happy to do this and can be relied upon to fulfil the role efficiently and effectively. Also, you have to ask whether he is ready to take on potential criminal liability for failing to do certain things as a landlord. In chapter 7 it was noted that there would be no CGT implications for you or your child if the house is in his name and he were resident, but your child will have to pay Income Tax on any rental income that is above his personal allowance, unless he chooses to take advantage of the Rent-a- Room scheme described above.

Using a property management company

Depending on circumstances it may be more sensible to use a property management company to look after your property. Property management companies offer advice on what needs to be done to your property to make it suitable for the rental market. They will collect the rent each month and provide you with a statement of account, visiting the property at agreed intervals to check that it is being well maintained. Also, they will arrange to have routine maintenance work carried out, after agreeing expenditure with you, and respond to the tenants' enquiries, problems and emergencies. Prices vary considerably so you should shop around for the best deal. If you decide to use a property management company, find out whether they are a member of the National Approved Letting Scheme (NALS) as members have to adhere to certain standards of customer service and care (www.nalscheme.co.uk).

Author's note

Over the past three or four years we have been able to obtain some cheaper properties from parents who have been desperate to sell a house that they have bought for their student child. In most cases this has been before the end of their child's course. There have been a number of reasons for this desperation, but the most common is that they have found it much harder than they had expected to be a landlord. Problems mentioned include a constant battle to obtain rent, being on call 24 hours a day, sometimes for the most ridiculous reasons, such as a light bulb has blown, and having to deal with the aftermath of parties.

Now, perhaps due to the credit crunch, we are finding that more and more landlords are selling property in our local town and that, as a result, we have many more students contacting us looking for accommodation. Most of our rental accommodation is let as early as January for the start of the academic year the following September/October. This situation illustrates that, in certain parts of the country, demand is exceeding supply for rental accommodation, so if you have the money for a deposit and your research suggests that tenants are available, it could be a good time to enter the student market.

Protecting your property and investment

As a property investor you must make sure that both your property and your investment are protected. To do this you must arrange adequate insurance and choose your tenants wisely.

Arranging insurance

You will need to arrange buildings and contents insurance, and landlord's insurance if you are intending to let your property (see chapter 10). This type of insurance will cover you for loss of rent or damage caused by tenants and will help to protect your investment. Also, many universities will insist that you have employer's liability insurance that covers death or injury to anyone you employ to work on your property.

Children often don't understand the importance of arranging insurance and may see it as an unnecessary expense. However, you should make sure that all your child's belongings are fully insured. This is of particular importance if you are the sole owner of the property and you are charging your child rent, as his belongings will not be covered on your landlord's insurance. All other tenants will also have to arrange their own insurance to cover their personal belongings that they take away with them at the end of the tenancy.

Choosing tenants

When choosing your tenants you should obtain references or a letter from the university to make sure that they are studying at that institution. Also, you should obtain the name and address of their parents so that they can be contacted if problems arise, or so that you can pass the information on to utility companies if students leave without paying bills. This should stop utility companies chasing you, as the landlord, for arrears (see case study 4, below). More information about choosing the right tenants is provided in chapter 9.

CASE STUDY 4 – MR AND MRS FITZSIMMONS

In 2001, Anna Fitzsimmons obtained a place at Birmingham University to study English and Drama. Her parents felt that it would be a good investment to buy a property for their daughter while she was studying on the three-year course. They intended to sell the house at the end of the course because it was their daughter's intention to work in London once she had completed her studies. Although they hadn't conducted any research, they 'felt' that it would be a good three-year investment.

Mr and Mrs Fitzsimmons lived in Kent and had never been to Birmingham, apart from a visit to the university with their daughter in the previous year. They travelled to Birmingham in May 2001 to find a house for Anna before she started in October. As they did not know the area, they visited local estate agents and asked about the best places to buy. At the time they felt that they did not want to contact the university accommodation office because they thought they would avoid the 'typical' student areas as they felt they would be 'too rough', even though they intended to let rooms to other students.

'This was our first mistake,' recalls Mrs Fitzsimmons. 'Why on earth we decided to avoid student areas I just don't know. Really I don't. Our second mistake was we started looking far too late. We found somewhere in July, but it took nearly four months to complete because there were some problems with the title deeds. Anna couldn't move into halls because they would only provide a contract for the whole year. And she couldn't find a room with other students because they had all gone house searching way before the summer vacation. In the end she had to go into bed and breakfast accommodation which cost us an arm and a leg.'

Anna was able to move into the new house in mid-November, four weeks after her course had started. She found this very disruptive to her studies, but was pleased to be in her own place, finally. However, her parents were unable to find students for the other three rooms because all the students had already found their accommodation. Mr and Mrs Fitzsimmons had to find tenants as soon as possible because they had to cover the mortgage on the property, so they advertised in the local press. As they lived and worked in Kent they were unable to deal with enquiries and visits from prospective tenants. This had to be done by Anna, who found it daunting and disrupting.

After three weeks of meeting with possible tenants, none of whom were suitable, Anna pleaded with her parents to delay finding tenants until she had made some friends and persuaded them to move in with her. They agreed, but had to cover the mortgage themselves until the following October, which meant that they didn't receive any rent for a whole year on the property. Luckily, they had enough savings to cover the loss. However, the following summer term Anna was unable to persuade her friends to move in with her because she lived so far from the university and none of them had cars.

Her parents could not afford to cover the rent for another year, so advertised their accommodation in the local paper, pointing out that only students need apply. Again, Anna had to meet with prospective tenants and, eventually, chose three people who could move in to her house.

'It was a nightmare,' recalls Anna. 'Mum and Dad had advertised for students. All I did was ask them where they were studying. I stupidly didn't ask for any proof. With hindsight I'm not sure two of them were students. They stayed around the house all day, they partied all night. They smoked even though I asked them not to. I couldn't get the rent off them. And they didn't pay any bills. And the telephone bill was enormous because they were always on the Net. I told Mum and Dad and eventually they came to visit and told them they had to pay what they owed. They said they would, but when I came back from uni the next day they'd gone. And they'd pinched my TV. Then I got a red electricity bill and they were threatening to cut me off. I'd not paid because I was trying to get the money off them. Mum and Dad paid it for me. The other tenant was OK, he paid on time, but he kept himself to himself. I never saw him really. It was so stressful and it made it really hard to concentrate on my uni work.'

Once the two tenants had left the property, Anna's parents were in the same situation. Term had started and they couldn't find other students for their property. Anna refused to advertise for other tenants, yet her parents realised that they could not continue to make such a loss. They decided that the only option was to sell.

'In the end we almost broke even, purely because house prices had risen in the area. But Anna had to leave the house just before we exchanged contracts, which was two weeks into January. Luckily, one of her friends had a spare room otherwise I don't know where she would have ended up. I would never do that again. It was so stressful and so disruptive to her studies, as she says. The main problem was that we lived so far away and couldn't help with running the property. Also, we were silly. We thought we could just do this and it would all work well. We just made so many mistakes.'

Asked what she would do differently next time, Mrs Fitzsimmons replied,

'Well, I probably wouldn't do it. But if I had to, I would speak to the people at the university accommodation office and I would ask for their advice and I would buy in a place they suggested. I would start looking much, much earlier. But that's hard when you only know your child's got a place in May and term starts in September. Also, I would make everyone sign a contract and I would make sure they were really students. Oh, and I would insist on their parents' addresses, in fact, I would want to meet their parents. But to be honest, I just wouldn't do it at all unless Anna had decided to study here in Canterbury. That would be different because we live here and I know the place. That would make a difference, I think. But really, honestly, it was too much trouble for us. I just don't think we're cut out for that kind of thing.'

Summary

Buying accommodation for student children is becoming increasingly popular as house prices continue to rise along with the rising costs of further and higher education. Through careful investment it is possible to provide a safe and secure house in which your child can live while he studies and make a decent profit from your investment. However, you must undertake thorough and systematic research, and understand your role as landlord, if you are to avoid the type of problems outlined above. It is important that you speak to the university accommodation officer so that you understand the rules and regulations associated with student lets. If you or your child is unable to manage the property, you will need to find a reliable property management company.

Some parents decide that they would like to invest in another property for their children well before they reach college or university age. This may be to sell when their child reaches a significant age, or to keep as a place in which their child can live when he leaves home. This type of property investment is discussed in the following chapter.

CHAPTER 9

Investing in a second property for your child

The Direct Line UK Second Property Index reveals that in 2006 there were 2.6 million second properties in the UK (www.directline.com). Its research shows that, in the five years from 2001, this figure has risen by 2.3 million. This indicates that buying a second property has become incredibly popular over recent years, with the greatest rise occurring in the buy-to-let market and in the 'handout home' market, where a property is bought by one person for the use of another. The Index predicts that the growth in the number of second properties will outstrip that of first-time purchases over the coming decade.

Parents, and in some cases grandparents, are finding that it is a worthwhile investment to buy a second home for their child or grandchild as this provides financial security for the future. Also, the child will have somewhere to live if he is unable to buy a property when he is old enough, especially if house prices continue to rise as they have done over the last few decades.

If you are interested in this type of investment, you need to consider the advantages and disadvantages, understand the financial implications, find suitable accommodation, manage the property and protect your investment. These issues are discussed in this chapter.

Assessing the advantages and disadvantages

The advantages and disadvantages inherent in this type of investment depend, in part, on the type of second-property investment in which you wish to become involved. This type of investment could include a holiday home to let to holidaymakers, either in the UK or abroad; a home that you let to tenants until your child reaches a significant age; or house in which you hope your child will live when he leaves home. Some of the advantages and disadvantages of buying a buy-to-let property are outlined in Table 5 (see chapter 8). Other advantages and disadvantages of investing in a second property are outlined in Table 8 below.

TABLE 8: THE ADVANTAGES AND DISADVANTAGES OF INVESTING IN A SECOND PROPERTY FOR YOUR CHILD

ADVANTAGES	DISADVANTAGES
Second-property ownership is becoming increasingly popular as there are large profits to be made with wise investment. There are good, competitive mortgages available on second properties, even in times of market uncertainty if you can pay a large deposit.	You can make a loss on your investment if you choose the wrong property, wrong location or pay too much when prices are falling. Failure to monitor the local and national housing market can lead to financial loss. Choosing the wrong mortgage for the market conditions and your personal circumstances could have a detrimental influence on your investment.
House prices continue to rise in holiday property hotspots.	Failure to recognise holiday property hotspots can lead to unwise purchasing choices and financial loss. Some people buy property in their favourite holiday destination without realising that it is not popular with other holidaymakers or that there is no market for holiday lets in the area.
If house prices rise, there are profits to be made	Empty properties attract vandals, burglars and squatters. It can be costly, time-

even if the property remains empty.	consuming and stressful to repair damage, evict squatters, arrange insurance and maintain empty properties.
Your child will have somewhere to live, no matter how much house prices rise in the future.	Your child may not like your choice of property and/or location. There may be arguments if your child wants to sell and you want to keep the property. If you have bought a property in a holiday hotspot, your child may not be too keen to make it a permanent home.
Equity release plans and remortgaging opportunities enable you to make use of equity tied up in your property to invest in another property, thus increasing opportunities for financial growth.	Poor advice and/or bad decisions can mean that you take out unsuitable equity release plans or mortgages that lead to financial loss and this could be on both your first and second property. Some of these products are unsuitable for older borrowers. You risk losing both homes if you cannot keep up with mortgage payments. Your child may be saddled with your debts when you die.
The overseas holiday home market has expanded rapidly and can provide good investment opportunities and a holiday home abroad for you and your family.	Unwise choices can lead to financial loss, especially if your chosen country experiences economic instability, political problems or a market crash. Your family may not want to visit the same place each year. It can be costly, time-consuming and difficult to manage a property abroad, if you are unable to find the right local help. Local tax and inheritance rules may mean that you are able to leave less money to your children.

As with all investments of this type it is important to seek professional advice that takes into account your financial circumstances and family situation if you are to avoid some of the problems outlined above. Also, issues of property management and protection are of particular importance if you are considering becoming a second homeowner (see below).

Understanding the financial implications

Before you decide to buy a second home as an investment for your child, you need to understand the financial implications of your decision. Chapter 6 offers advice about planning your finances and understanding the costs involved with purchasing property. The tax implications of property transactions are discussed in chapter 5, although you should note that any foreign tax implications are outside the scope of this book. In addition to this advice, it is important to consider ways to raise capital, tax implications on holiday lets and ways to protect your property investment.

Mortgages

There are a wide variety of mortgages available for people who wish to buy a second home in the UK, including buy-to-let mortgages, second-home mortgages, holiday let mortgages, remortgages and self-certification mortgages. Most banks and building societies will look favourably on borrowers who have paid off their mortgage recently or have fewer debts, more savings and higher incomes.

If you do decide to take out a mortgage on a second property, you should avoid borrowing more than 90 per cent. Indeed, you will only be able to borrow this amount in today's economic climate if you are perceived to be a low risk borrower, that is you have a stable, regular income and have paid off or have a very small mortgage on your main property. If you are able to borrow less than 90 per cent, you will avoid having to pay an expensive mortgage indemnity premium (MIP). This is also known as a mortgage indemnity guarantee (MIG) and is an insurance premium that protects the lender if you default on the loan. This is relevant with any second property that you buy, including a home for your student child (see chapter 8) or if you decide to take out a joint mortgage with your child (see chapter 7). If you are able to put down a deposit of at least 10 per cent on your investment property, you should not be charged this premium.

It is possible to obtain a lifetime mortgage that enables you to take out a loan on your property to raise a lump sum that you can spend as you choose. The interest is higher than with an ordinary loan and is repaid from the sale of your home on your death or the death of your spouse if he survives you. With this type of scheme any loss that is made on the sale of your property is borne by the company that arranged the plan rather than by your heirs or estate. However, if the loan value plus interest is less than the sale proceeds, the excess goes into your estate to be distributed according to your Will. It is possible to arrange to take the equity in stages, if this is preferable, which is known as a drawdown lifetime mortgage. You should note that lifetime mortgages are a lifetime commitment and if you change your mind you may have to pay a substantial Early Repayment Charge. Professional advice should be sought if you feel that this type of product may be appropriate for your needs.

There are a variety of mortgage comparison websites that enable you to compare and contrast the best mortgage deals. These include www.moneymadeclear.fsa.gov.uk, www.moneysupermarket.com, www. fool.co.uk/mortgages and www.moneynet.co.uk. Shop around for the best deals and make sure that any lender you choose is an FSA regulated firm by checking the Register at www.fsa.gov.uk/register.

Mortgages for overseas properties

If you are hoping to buy a second home abroad, you can take out a mortgage on the overseas property through a UK lender, or you can choose to arrange a mortgage in the country in which the property is located. UK, US, Euro and multi-currency mortgages are available, but you need to monitor exchange rates and currency fluctuations to make sure that you obtain the best deal for your circumstances. In general, it's a good idea to take the loan out in the currency that matches the income used to source the loan, so if a holiday rent is paid in Euros, you should use a Euro loan. This removes the risk of currency movement from the investment, unless of course you wish to dabble in currency arbitrage, where you take advantage of divergences in exchange rates in different money markets by buying a currency in one market and selling it in another market.

Different countries have different rules about how much you can borrow, the age of borrowers, proof of income and maximum terms, so you will need to obtain local, professional advice.

Equity release plans

Releasing equity in your current home may help you to raise cash to pay a larger deposit on your second home. There are a variety of equity release plans available for people who want to take advantage of the value of their home without selling, and some of these are described in chapter 7. However, all equity release plans of this type should be approached with caution as you risk giving up a considerable amount of equity in return for what can be a small amount of money. An alternative option may be to downsize to release the equity in your house (see chapter 4).

If you are thinking about equity release plans to help you buy a second home, you must seek specialist advice and use a reputable organisation. Also, you must discuss all your plans with your children when they are old enough to understand the implications of your decisions. More information about equity release plans can be obtained from Safe Home Income Plans (SHIP) (www.ship-ltd.org). All SHIP plans carry a 'no negative equity' guarantee, which means that you will never owe more than the value of your home.

Tax on UK holiday lettings

HM Revenue & Customs recognises income from a UK holiday let as earned income. This is different to income generated from other types of property letting that are classed as investment income, or unearned income. This means that there are different rules concerning tax on income generated from holiday lets. Your second property will be defined as a holiday let if it meets the following conditions:

- It is in the UK.

- It is fully furnished.

- Iit is available for holiday lettings to the public for at least 140 days a year.

- It is let as a holiday let for at least 70 days a year to paying customers who pay a full market rate, rather than to family or friends for a nominal rate or free of charge.

- The holiday lets must be lets of no more than 31 days in length.

- The holiday lets must be the only type of lets for at least 210 days in any one year (211 days in a leap year). There are no restrictions on longer lets in the remaining 155 days but these longer lets do not count as holiday lets.

If your second home meets these conditions, you can take advantage of certain types of tax relief on your property; for example, any loss that you make on your property can be offset against your other income and, as this includes other income that is not related to your property income, you may be able to reduce your overall tax bill. Or, if it is preferable, you can carry the loss forward and offset it against future letting profits. If you are married, you can maximise tax allowances by having the property in the name of the lower earner. This is useful if the lower earner is in the lower rate tax band and the higher earner is in the higher band, unless you are losing money on the property, in which case it is better in the name of the higher earner. Alternatively, you could consider buying the property in your child's name, which may save on certain taxes (see chapter 7).

When you come to sell your holiday property you may be able to take advantage of CGT relief, such as 'business rollover relief'. This means that, if you reinvest your money in another UK holiday letting property within three years, and that property costs the same or more than the property you have sold, you may be able to defer payment of CGT until you sell the new property. This relief enables you to reinvest all of the proceeds of the sale in a replacement property, which you would not be able to do if you had to pay a tax liability. This relief can also be used to avoid paying CGT on sales of other types of business, where the proceeds are invested in a holiday letting business. This type of relief is useful if you are hoping to establish and build up a holiday letting business as an investment for your child. However, the rules and regulations can be complex, so if you are thinking about taking advantage of this relief you might find it useful to seek advice from an accountant or tax adviser. More information about tax advantages on UK holiday lettings can be obtained from www.hmrc.gov.uk.

Finding suitable properties

Appendices 2 and 3 offer general advice about searching for and viewing potential properties. In addition to this advice, there are other issues which you should be aware of when finding suitable accommodation. These depend on the type of second property in which you are interested, as discussed below.

UK holiday accommodation for your family

If you are thinking about buying a holiday home in the UK for you and your family, and using this property as an investment for your children when they get older, there are several points that you should consider when choosing and buying a property. These include the following:

- Is the area a popular holiday property spot? Savills Residential Research suggests that the most popular areas for this type of accommodation in the UK are the South West, the South and the East Anglia coast, although there are some areas that are more popular than others located within these regions (www.savills.co.uk).

- Is there plenty of private and public investment in the area? Is the area displaying signs of ongoing regeneration and development?

- Is the property market buoyant in the area and is it likely to remain that way for the duration of your investment? Will you be able to sell the property for a profit? Is demand high for that type of property in that area? Will it remain so in the future? Although you cannot predict what will happen in the future, you can make sound judgements based on careful research (see chapter 1).

- Are there any plans, schemes or development issues that could have either a negative or positive influence on the price of the property? Consult the planning department at the local authority for more information.

- Are you and your family happy to holiday in this region each year?

- Is it safe and secure to leave your accommodation empty? An informal discussion with the local crime prevention officer will help with your research.

- Is there any risk of flooding or evidence of subsidence? If so, you may find it difficult to obtain insurance for your holiday home or you will have to pay a much higher premium.

UK holiday accommodation to let

In addition to the points outlined above, you should think about the following points if you are hoping to let your UK holiday accommodation:

- Is there demand for this type of holiday let in this area? Obtain more information and advice from other landlords and letting agents that specialise in holiday lets.

- What prices can you charge for the accommodation? How much do other landlords charge?

- How long is the holiday season in the area? Is there potential to let the accommodation out of season? Are attractions, services and facilities open all year, or does everything close down out of season? The tourist information office should be able to help with your research.

- Who will look after the accommodation when it is empty? Who will service the accommodation between lets? How much will their services cost? How will this affect your profits?

Author's note

Our friends own a holiday home in the Isle of Wight that they bought as an investment for their children. They intended to visit the house during the school holidays and let the property for the rest of the year. However, they soon found that they were unable to do this. The size of the house meant that it was popular with families, yet families only wanted the property during the school holidays. Our friends found that they could not visit their property as much as they wished, because they had to let it to holidaymakers. They decided that they would keep two weeks for themselves at the end of the summer holiday, but found that most of the time was spent tidying and decorating after the summer lets.

Now that their children have grown up the family rarely visit the property. They intend to sell when the last child reaches the age of 30. (They believe this is a good age for their children to receive the profits from the property, as they should be settled into their working lives and hopefully will not squander the money.)

Overseas holiday accommodation

You may decide to buy a property overseas as an investment for your child and a holiday home for your family. If you choose this option, you should seek specialist advice as there are a number of factors you need to consider. It is imperative that you are clear about the type of investment that you want, and that you understand how this will influence the financial performance of your investment. This involves an assessment of the following:

- Buying a house abroad means that you are investing in the property market, a foreign economy and undertaking some currency arbitrage. Are you happy to do this and do you understand the implications for your family and finances?

- Some countries have different laws about property inheritance and your children may have to pay IHT in the UK and the country in which the property is located. Do you understand these laws and the financial implications for your investment?

- Are you investing in an appreciating property or perhaps taking a gamble on a developing country? These are different types of investment and you need to be clear about the type that suits you. Also, can you be sure that the country in which you buy is going to remain stable, politically and economically?

If you decide to buy abroad, you should consider the following points when finding suitable properties:

- Is the location well served by a UK airport? Are cheap flights available? Are cheap flights available all year? Is the destination airport open all year?

- Does the property need renovating and refurbishing? Are you able to spend the time doing the work or overseeing workers? Do you have good contacts in the area, or can you build up these contacts? Will language be an issue?

- Are all the legal documents in order? Were the necessary planning permissions sought for the development? Recent media coverage suggests that some people buying abroad are losing their property and investment because new developments did not have the required permission. You must seek specialist, independent legal advice before buying.

- Is the property well served by public transport?

- Are prices rising in the country and are they likely to continue doing so? Is the country popular with other nationalities or is the property market being kept afloat by UK buyers? What would happen if UK buyers lost interest? If the property market in the UK suffers, people are likely to sell their properties abroad and this could affect your investment if you don't choose your property wisely.

- Who will look after your property when you are not in the country? Is there a local individual or company that you could trust to take on the role?

- Would you be able to let the property if required? Are similar properties available in the area? Are these let easily? What prices are charged? Would this cover your mortgage? Would you be able to find someone reliable to service the accommodation between lets?

- How long is the holiday season? Would the area be popular with holidaymakers and/or your family out of season? Are weather conditions favourable all year? Have you visited the area at different times of the year?

The Federation of Overseas Property Developers, Agents and Consultants (FOPDAC) was established in 1973 to work with members and protect the interests of people buying overseas property. It has recently merged with the National Association of Estate Agents (overseas) (NAEA) and both organisations have a Code of Ethics to which members must adhere. When obtaining information and advice about overseas property, and when searching for a property, you should use an organisation that is a member of FOPDAC or NAEA as it should work within this Code to provide the best possible service to the customer (www.naea.co.uk).

Author's note

I have a friend who has recently bought an investment property in Turkey. She bought the property over the Internet from a developer who was building a large complex set around three swimming pools. She viewed the plans, paid her deposit and waited for the developer to notify her when it was finished.

My friend had no intention of visiting the property, believing that a local company could furnish and let the accommodation. However, the prices that she was quoted for this service were far too high, so she decided to visit Turkey and furnish the property herself. When she arrived she found that the balcony and small garden were backed up against a three-metre-high wall, which contained the swimming pool. There was no view or access to the pool from her apartment. Obviously, the plans had been very misleading – they showed that the balcony and garden were located against the edge of the pool, but did not show this massive drop in ground level. My friend argued with the developer and eventually managed to obtain a better property on the site. However, if she had not visited the apartment herself, this major problem would not have been identified until it was too late.

A home for your child

When buying a home that your child can live in when he is older, it is hard to know what type of accommodation will be suitable, as you cannot predict his wants and needs for the future. Indeed, you may have to be flexible in your investment and enable your child to make decisions about whether he lives in the property or chooses to sell. Despite the unpredictability of this type of investment, there are a number of points that you should consider when looking for suitable properties:

• Will the property be safe and secure for your child?

• Is it located close to other family property? Although your child may not want to live close to you on a permanent basis, it would provide him with security and familiarity when he first leaves home.

• Will he be able to find employment and/or study opportunities close by?

• Is it well served by public transport and does it have private parking?

- Is there anything in the local authority development plan that may have a detrimental effect on your investment? (A development plan is a set of documents that set out the policies and proposals for the development and use of land within the local authority. You can access information about your local authority development plan by contacting them direct or visiting www.planningportal.gov.uk.)

- Are there any environmental factors that could affect your investment, such as flooding, pollution, airport extensions or proposed mobile mast installations? Visit www.environment-agency.gov.uk for information about flooding potential and www.sitefinder.ofcom.org.uk for information about mobile masts.

- Are there any highways planned that could devalue your property in the future? Visit the Highways Agency website to browse road projects by region and for detailed information about each project, whether planned, current or completed: www.highways.gov.uk.

Buy-to-let accommodation

One of the best ways to find suitable buy-to-let accommodation is to get to know the area thoroughly and find out more about the other landlords. Many local authorities have a local landlord's group, which is an ideal place to network and meet other people who are experienced in the buy-to-let market. Through networking in this way you can visit other properties and get to know what is available, the prices that can be charged and the type of problems that you may encounter when letting your property. Further advice about finding suitable buy-to-let property is offered in chapter 8.

A property to sell

Some parents buy a property as an investment when their children are young that they hope to sell on when their child reaches a specific age. If this is the case, you need to consider how the property market is performing in that area and make predictions about how it will perform in the future, over both the short and the long term (see chapter 1). A useful price predicting tool is available on the 'Your Mortgage' website (www.yourmortgage.co.uk). More information about choosing suitable properties is provided above and in Appendices 2 and 3.

You also need to decide what you are going to do with the property until your child reaches the specific age that you have selected. If you are hoping to let the property, you should take note of the points listed above and the advice offered in chapter 8 when finding suitable properties. It is not advisable to buy a property and leave it empty, as empty properties attract vandals, burglars and squatters, and they are more expensive to insure. Too many empty properties in an area can also force prices down and irritate locals. Also, some local authorities are cracking down on the problem of empty homes and, if they are not being used and have been empty for a number of years, they may decide to acquire the property under a Compulsory Purchase Order so that it can be refurbished and sold or tenanted.

Making the most of your investment

All investors want to get the best possible return on their investment. To do this successfully you need to make sure that you buy the right property, for the right price in the right location, at the right time. This involves careful and systematic research into the local and national property market and being able to predict investment trends and prospects (see chapter 1). You also need to make sure that the location is suitable and that there are no planned developments that could have an adverse influence on your investment.

In the UK to find out useful information about the area in which the property is located visit http://neighbourhood.statistics.gov.uk/ dissemination and enter the postcode of the property in which you are interested. You can find out how the neighbourhood performs on topics such as crime, education and environment, and compare this to the performance of England as a whole.

If you are thinking about buying abroad, contact the British Embassy in the foreign country for more information about living there, crime levels, education and so on. A list of embassies can be obtained from the Foreign and Commonwealth Office (FCO) website (www.fco.gov.uk). This website also contains useful information on travelling and living abroad, with an alphabetical list of countries containing information about issues such as terrorism, crime, law and customs, health, money and visa requirements.

Fashions and trends

Another way that you can make the most of your investment is to take note of changing trends and buy or develop your investment property accordingly. For example, environmental issues are high on the political and public agendas at the moment. One way to make the most of your investment is by investing in an eco-friendly home, either in the UK or abroad, or by making eco-friendly improvements when you renovate or refurbish your property. This is because buyers are willing to spend more on a property that they perceive to be environmentally friendly. Also, eco-tourism is becoming more popular and you may find it easier to let your holiday accommodation if you can emphasise its green credentials. Comprehensive information about buying and investing in green property is available in another of my books *The Complete Guide to Buying, Selling and Investing in Green Property.*

Setting rent levels

An important part of property investment is to make sure that you receive the best possible rent for your property, whether you are letting on short-term tenancies or letting holiday accommodation in the UK or abroad. Perhaps surprisingly, when the property market begins to slow, rents can rise. This is because people delay buying a house until the market is more stable, or until prices have fallen to a level they can afford. Other people are reluctant to take on mortgage debt when they perceive the economy to be in crisis, and others sell their property and sit on the proceeds until they perceive the time is right to buy. All these people, some of whom will be high earners, will be looking for rented accommodation, which can push prices up. Indeed, Paragon Mortgages, a company that specialises in buy-to-let mortgages, believes that UK rents rose by 19 per cent in 2007.

Despite this rise in rents, many inexperienced investors bought the wrong type of property, in the wrong place at the wrong time for too high a price. This type of property includes inner city apartments that are expensive and difficult to let because there are not enough tenants available and rent levels are too high. Landlords have struggled to find tenants who are willing to pay the amount of rent that they need to cover the mortgage. Now, as the credit crunch begins to bite, many small-time investors are getting the jitters and pulling out, whereas others who have been unable to meet mortgage payments are losing their investment properties through repossession. This has led to recent media reports that the buy-to-let bubble has burst. However, experienced investors who are in for the long term are finding that this situation is helping their investment – there are more tenants chasing fewer properties and rents rise as a result. To be successful, you must make sure that you buy the right property, at the right time, in the right location and for the right price. You must also make sure that the tenants are available and willing to pay the amount of rent that you require to make your investment succeed. Checklists to help you do this are provided in Appendices 1–4.

When choosing a realistic rent to charge for your property you need to speak to other landlords and letting agents in the area to find out about rent levels. Try to view rented properties in the area to find out what rent is being charged for what standard of accommodation. Find out how long properties remain empty and how easy it is to find tenants. Landlord's associations or the local authority should be able to help you with this research for buy-to-let accommodation and the local tourist information office should be able to provide advice for holiday lets.

Managing your property

There are different management issues that you should be aware of, depending on the type of second property that you have bought.

Holiday lets

One of the biggest complaints made by holidaymakers is about the cleanliness of their accommodation. If you live at a distance from your second home, you will need to employ the services of a reliable person to clean your property and make sure that it is well presented in between lets. There are cleaning companies that specialise in holiday lets available in some of the more popular tourist areas, or you could choose to use a reliable individual, chosen on personal recommendation.

If you decide to clean your property yourself, you will have to make sure that you are always available during the changeover period. It is advisable to set rules about departure and arrival times so that you have enough time to clean and maintain the property to the required standard. Also, you should be aware of major issues that can cause problems with short-term lets, for example, discovering pests such as bedbugs or mice when cleaning for the next guests.

Whether you decide to use a cleaning company or an individual that has been recommended to you, it is advisable to visit the property on regular occasions between lets, until you are sure that the property is being managed in the way that you want. You may also find it useful to produce a short questionnaire that can be distributed to guests and alert you to problems that you are unaware of. If guests are unhappy with your property, you will not benefit from important repeat business and serious complaints can be costly, time-consuming and stressful to sort out. Again, comprehensive insurance will help to cover you against problems that can arise with letting holiday accommodation (see chapter 10).

Buy-to-let

If you are letting your property to tenants on a fixed-term contract, you should note that while your tenant is living in the property it is his home and he has the right of control over his accommodation. You must respect this and agree to conduct the repairs for which you are responsible. You will need to find out whether the repair work is necessary and if so, carry it out, or arrange for someone else to do so. If you fail to act on the information supplied by your tenant and do not carry out the required work, your tenant can sue you in court. If this happens, the court can award damages and order repairs to be done. You must provide your tenant with at least 24 hours' prior notice in writing if you want to access the property, or to send in builders or other workers, although this does not apply in emergencies.

If you choose to use a property management company, it will arrange for all necessary work to be carried out, once this has been agreed with you.

More information about using a property management company is provided in chapters 8 and 10.

Protecting your property

The type of protection that you will need depends on the type of second property investment, as discussed below.

Buy-to-let

If you are hoping to let your second property to tenants, you can protect your property and investment by making sure that you choose the right tenants, obtain references and draw up a legal tenancy agreement (see chapter 8). Choosing the right tenants involves six stages:

- **Stage 1:** choose the type of tenants you want and advertise accordingly. This will involve decisions about where you are going to position your property in the market. For example, for luxury accommodation you will want wealthy tenants, or corporate tenants; for middle range property you will be looking for professionals and working people; and for cheaper end property you will most likely be looking for the unemployed or students, etc. Whichever you choose you need to make sure that the market is available in your chosen location and advertise using a medium that will be accessed by your chosen market. Your advertisement should be well worded so that it is clear who should apply.

- **Stage 2:** make contact with prospective tenants and ask them a series of questions, such as name, contact address, reasons for moving, type of employment, whether they smoke, whether they have children and/or pets. Through careful observation and by listening to responses you will get a feel for whether a tenant is suitable. Reputable tenants will try to answer your questions fully and honestly.

- **Stage 3:** invite prospective tenants to view the property. While you are 'selling' the benefits of your property to them, you are also finding out whether they are suitable. Ask plenty of questions and listen carefully to their responses. If they bring a family member or friend with them, obtain more information from both people. Assess appearance, attitude, enthusiasm, reliability and the length of time it takes them to make a decision. Make sure you have a manual available with all the information that will be useful for the tenant, such as rubbish collection days, emergency telephone numbers and user manuals for appliances.

- **Stage 4:** ask the prospective tenant to complete an application form. This will include all personal contact details, names and addresses of referees and asks the tenant to confirm that he understands the terms and conditions under which the property is going to be let. If you are able to ask a number of tenants to complete an application form, you have the luxury of going through each to choose the tenant that you think will be most suitable for your property, once references and any other checks have been conducted.

- **Stage 5:** follow up references and carry out any other checks that may be necessary, such as contacting previous landlords. Don't rely on paper references that have been provided by the tenants themselves. Treat the selection process as if you are choosing an applicant for a job – you need to choose the best person who will cause the least amount of trouble. Once he has signed the agreement and has moved into your property he is protected by certain legal rights, so you need to make sure that you choose tenants who will look after your property and pay their rent on time, making your role as landlord much easier.

- **Stage 6:** ask your chosen tenant to sign your tenancy agreement. At this stage you should ask for identification and make sure that there is an independent witness present to sign the document.

Another important way to protect your property is to make sure that you arrange appropriate insurance (see chapter 10). This is of particular importance for properties that are let to tenants or holidaymakers or properties that remain empty for short periods of time.

Author's note

When we first began to let our accommodation we thought we wouldn't have the luxury of being able to pick and choose tenants. However, we soon learnt that we needed to spend a lot of time choosing the right people because this would save time, money and stress in the long run.

In the first year we had problems with tenants not paying rent and leaving the property without paying bills; in some cases we had to take them to court to get them out of our property. Nobody likes doing this and it was stressful for our whole family. We learnt fairly quickly that choosing your tenants carefully, and refusing unsuitable applicants, is of paramount importance. Now we follow the stages described above with every potential new tenant. It might seem a long process, but it is certainly worth it.

Holiday lets

If you are hoping to let holiday accommodation, you must arrange adequate insurance to protect your investment. This includes buildings and contents insurance, which will cover the structure and contents of the building; public liability, which will cover you for civil actions brought by guests who may sustain injury on your property; employee liability, which is a legal requirement if you employ casual labour; loss of rental income cover and cancellation insurance. You may also need to arrange your motor insurance for business use if you use your vehicle for your holiday letting business. More information about the different types of insurance is offered in chapter 10.

Although you may not have the luxury of picking and choosing your guests, you should do all you can to make sure that you choose reliable people who will respect your property and enjoy their holiday, especially as repeat business is so important. This involves the following:

- Obtain a name, address and contact number.

- Ask for a deposit and make sure that potential guests are clear about the situations in which this might, or might not, be refundable.

- Provide clear details about when you will require full payment. It is up to you to decide whether you will refund payment if your guests are unable to take up the accommodation due to unforeseen circumstances.

- Be professional at all times. If you produce professional looking literature and act professionally, guests are more likely to treat your accommodation with respect.

- Make sure your accommodation is clean and tidy. Again, this tends to lead to more respect.

- Be honest in your advertising. Don't be tempted to exaggerate, tell lies or hide the truth as this can annoy guests.

- Remove any personal belongings that have sentimental value or any real monetary value. However, 'homely' touches can increase your guests' enjoyment without costing you a lot of money.

Overseas property

If you decide to buy a second property overseas, then there are some additional protection issues which you should be aware of. These include the following:

- Never sign a contract written in a language with which you are unfamiliar. Always seek specialist language help and advice.

- Seek specialist advice from an independent, local solicitor, architect, surveyor and mortgage adviser as they will understand the rules, regulations and laws. Make sure people you take advice from are members of a reputable professional body.

- Always have an independent survey carried out on the property and seek specialist opinions on problems that are highlighted in the survey. It is best to use individuals or companies that are independent of the organisation that is selling the property.

- Make sure that you do not inherit any debt with the property. This could be due to unpaid property tax for which you, as the new owner, could be liable. This could also occur if you have bought a plot on a new development and the developer has borrowed money and used each individual plot as security against the loan.

- Make sure that you know about, understand and can pay all local taxes, as failure to do so could lead to court action and seizure of your overseas property. You might find it useful to set up standing orders from a local bank account to make sure that these bills are covered.

- Make sure that your property is comprehensively insured and that you disclose the correct use of the property, which may include periods of letting and periods when the property remains empty. Insurance can be arranged in the UK if language barriers are an issue.

Summary

Buying a second home is becoming increasingly popular amongst parents who see this type of ownership as a good investment for their child. Some decide to buy a holiday home in the UK or abroad, whereas others decide to buy a property that they hope their child will live in when he is older. Although it is difficult to know where your child will want to live when he leaves home, there are certain considerations that will make your decisions easier, such as buying a property near your family home, which can help to provide security and a familiar environment for your child. As with all types of property investment, comprehensive market research is vital if your investment is to be successful and enjoyable; for example, you must make sure that there are no environmental factors, such as flooding, or proposed developments, such as a new highway, which will have a negative impact on your investment. You can obtain this information from the Environment Agency and from the Highways Agency (see above).

If you have decided that investing in a second property is a useful way to invest in your child's future, you need to make sure that you protect your investment. This includes protection against unforeseen and unplanned circumstances, and the maintenance and management of your property so that you can increase the profit obtained on your investment. These issues are discussed in the next chapter.

Part 3:
Protecting your investment

CHAPTER 10

Protecting against financial loss

Investing in property for your child is a long-term investment during which time the housing market and economy can experience significant fluctuations that could seriously affect your financial investment. If you are to make a sound investment, you need to keep abreast of these fluctuations and know if and when to change your investment strategy. Advice on how to do this was offered in chapter 1.

In addition to monitoring the property market and economy, you also need to make sure that your investment property is well maintained and managed so that the value of your property rises and your child's inheritance grows in the way that you intend. It is also important that your property and your financial investment are thoroughly protected against unforeseen and unplanned problems and that you know when and how to sell to maximise your profits. These issues are discussed in this chapter.

Maintaining your property

All investment property has to be well maintained if you are to maximise your profits and protect your investment. Problems that are not dealt with as soon as they occur can cause serious damage that is expensive and time-consuming to rectify. If your investment property is tenanted, you should include a clause in your contract that states that tenants must notify you as soon as problems occur and you should act on this information as soon as possible (see chapters 8 and 9).

Using builders and service providers

Get to know local, reliable tradespeople and service providers. Speak to other landlords to obtain recommendations and don't be tempted to use people who cold call. Always obtain a written estimate for any work you require and ask for quotations from three different companies, following up references and inspecting previous work, if possible. For small and large domestic building work you can download a Plain English Contract from the Federation of Master Builders' (FMB) website (www.fmb.org.uk). The builder does not have to be a member of the FMB to use the contract, but it is advisable to use a member as the FMB sets high standards that builders must meet in order to become members. Also, they have a useful dispute resolution procedure that you can take advantage of if things go wrong. You can find contact details of a member in your area by using the online directory.

When arranging for work to be carried out on your property you will need to make sure that the appropriate rules and regulations are followed, such as building regulations, listed building consent, the Party Wall Act 1996 and electrical regulations. More information about all these rules and regulations can be obtained from *The Complete Guide to Property Development for Small Investors* (details in Further Reading).

When you are happy with the work provided by builders, tradespeople and service providers, tell them so and ask if they are happy to work for you again. This way, you can build up a list of reliable people who will be able to help you to maintain your property at short notice and if emergencies should occur. Also, when you come to sell your property, you will find it useful to have obtained Guarantee Protection Insurance (GPI) for certain types of work that have been undertaken on your property. This is specialist insurance cover which relates to the property rather than the owner and can provide peace of mind for new owners of the property. More information about GPI is provided below.

Using a property maintenance company

You can choose to use a property maintenance company if you live at a distance from the property, if you are not competent in doing the work yourself, or if you are unsure about employing builders and tradespeople. Good companies will be able to cover all the work you require, such as fixing and clearing gutters, small building work, roof repairs, carpentry, joinery and plumbing, although you should check that they are qualified to carry out plumbing and/or electrical work. You should also check that they are members of the relevant professional association, such as the FMB (www.fmb.org.uk), and that they have comprehensive insurance to cover their work. Ask to see their public liability insurance certificate and check that all jobs they carry out for you have the necessary warranties and guarantees. You should include all guarantees, warranties and completion certificates in your Home Information Pack as these will be a useful selling point when you come to dispose of your property at a later date.

When choosing a property maintenance company, ask for references from previous satisfied customers and try to speak to these customers and inspect the maintenance work, if possible. If you join a local landlord's group, you can obtain recommendations for companies in the area. Once you have built up a good relationship with a local company you should be able to rely on it to carry out work quickly, efficiently and in emergencies. Also, it should be able to make sure that all the work is carried out following the correct procedures and with the appropriate permissions and consents.

Author's note

It has taken us a long time, but we now have a list of people we can call upon in an emergency. It gives us peace of mind to know that these people will be reliable and won't rip us off in an emergency. Some of the people we employ have become good friends over the years – my brother and sister were recently asked to be witnesses at our electrician's wedding.

Arranging insurance

Relevant insurance is extremely important for your investment property. It will help protect you against problems such as floods, fire, storm, burglary, loss of rent, death or injury to workers or tenants and legal action.

There are various types of insurance and you should think carefully about what you need before you decide to buy. There are a number of insurance comparison websites that enable you to both compare and contrast deals. Four well-known and reputable insurance comparison sites are www.confused.com, www.moneysupermarket.com, www.comparethe market.com and www.insurancewide.com. These provide a useful starting point for your research into the best insurance deals on the market. When searching for insurance work out exactly what you need, don't be tempted to buy unnecessary insurance and make sure that you are covered for everything you require. When you have obtained a quotation find out what extras are included and remove those that you don't need as your premium could be reduced further.

You should try several comparison sites as different insurers offer the best deals to different sites, and some of the better known sites often have very good deals that you might not be able to obtain direct with the insurance company. Also, deals change from year to year, so you can save money by switching your policy on an annual basis. However, you should make sure that you are completely covered, rather than choose the cheapest deal. Policies and excess amounts vary considerably, so check all the small print before you buy.

Buildings insurance

Your mortgage company will insist that you take out buildings insurance and it may try to direct you to its own insurance cover. However, you should shop around as you should be able to find a better deal elsewhere.

Buildings insurance is available for the structure of your property and for permanent fixtures and fittings, which often include sub-structures such as garages, greenhouses and sheds.

Coverage usually includes loss or damage as a result of weather, natural disasters, purposeful harm and accidents, to both the interior and exterior of the building. You should take out buildings insurance from the first day you accept responsibility or ownership of the property and you will need to make sure that you make a detailed declaration about how the building is to be used, especially if it is to be let to tenants or holidaymakers. If your child is buying the property in his name, you must stress the importance of this type of insurance and make sure that his property is fully covered from the day he exchanges contracts. He will also need to let the insurance company know if he intends to take in lodgers.

If you or your child has to make a claim on your buildings insurance, keep all details, including dates, about the type of claim and the cost of the claim as you will have to disclose this information when you take out buildings insurance over the next three or five years, depending on the company that you choose.

Many companies will offer a combination of buildings and contents insurance which is usually cheaper than two separate policies.

Contents insurance

Contents insurance will cover the value of possessions or property in the event of damage, destruction or loss. This includes all non-permanent structures and fixtures in your investment property, as well as furniture and appliances. Items that are of particular value will need to be named separately on your policy. Policies can be extended to include accidental damage, which is a good option for high risk individuals and families, such as those with children and pets. The policy should cover the cost of replacing your possessions, not the current value of the items.

If you are to become a landlord, you can arrange contents insurance to cover fixtures, fittings and possessions that are left in the property. Tenants will need to arrange their own insurance to cover their personal possessions. If your investment property has been bought in your child's name and he arranges his own contents insurance, his possessions will be covered in his property. However, if your child is renting a room from you, he will have to take separate insurance for his personal belongings. This may also be the case even if he is not paying you any rent and living in your investment property – you should check with your insurer as individual policies will vary. Certain types of landlord's insurance will provide contents cover within the policy (see below) so you should check that you do not waste your money by taking out unnecessary insurance.

Life assurance

Life assurance is a policy that is taken out to cover the eventual death of the insured. It can also be known as 'whole of life' insurance. It is insurance against an event that will happen and therefore is not term limited and payment on death is guaranteed, if you meet all the conditions laid out in the small print. Some life assurance policies can include payments in cases of critical illness and accident. The cost of coverage depends on a number of factors, including your age, health, lifestyle and occupation.

It is possible to use life assurance policies in the following ways:

- to reduce the value of your estate on death by paying premiums into your policy up to your annual exemption (£3,000) into a policy;

- as a method of funding IHT liability on your death in circumstances where assets may not be easily released; for example, market conditions are not right to sell an investment property to fund IHT;

- to cover your children's IHT liability in cases where, for example, they might have to sell the family home to pay the tax bill.

Although life assurance benefits are generally free of deductions for personal Income Tax, in the event of your death, the proceeds usually form part of your estate and therefore could be liable to IHT. However, it is possible to place your life assurance policy in trust, which means that the benefits are paid to the trust and not to your estate. Through placing your policy in trust you can make sure that there is no IHT liability and ensure that the money goes to your children quickly, without the delay of probate. Often all that is required is to complete a simple form of trust provided by your insurers, on which you name your beneficiaries. However, there are different types of trust that you can use, depending on your needs and circumstances. This includes bare trusts and interest in possession trusts and these are discussed in chapter 12. (You may need to set up a trust to protect your life assurance funds in cases of separation or divorce, for example.) Trust rules and regulations can be complex, so if you wish to follow this route you should seek independent trust advice, tailored to your specific needs.

Life insurance

Life insurance is different in that it covers the possible event of death during a specified period of time. This type of insurance can also be known as 'level term' or 'mortgage protection' insurance. You will need to take out life insurance when you take out a mortgage as it will cover you in cases of unexpected death during the term of your mortgage. This is especially useful if you take out a second mortgage on an investment property which your children or spouse may struggle to repay if you died unexpectedly.

Your child should be encouraged to take out this insurance if he is buying the property in his own name. This is of particular importance if you have invested money in the property. Premiums depend on your risk factors, or those of your child. It is important to check the small print with this type of insurance as certain exclusions may apply. On this type of policy you simply need to name your beneficiaries on the form supplied by your insurer.

Also, you can take out this type of policy to cover your children's IHT liability on your death if you have made a large gift (over the exempt IHT amount) within the previous seven years. This type of insurance is known as a 'gift inter vivos' policy and it will run for seven years. The policy should be set up in trust to ensure that the funds fall outside your estate for IHT purposes.

Income protection

This insurance can also be called accident, sickness and unemployment insurance and it provides cover if you are unable to work due to illness or accident. Most policies will enable you to insure for 50–60 per cent of your earnings before tax and will pay out a regular tax-free income in cases of illness or disability. This is useful insurance cover if you have monthly outgoings on an investment property that could not be met by statutory sick pay, employers' insurance or other insurance policies. Also, this type of insurance may be useful for your child if he has taken out a mortgage in his own name. The cost of monthly premiums will depend on your risk factors and the deferred period that you choose. This is the length of time that can occur between making a claim and receiving a payment.

Mortgage payment protection insurance

This is a comprehensive insurance policy that will cover your mortgage repayments over a specified length of time if you are unable to meet the payments yourself. This could be due to accident, disability, illness or unemployment. If you are taking a second mortgage on a property, this type of cover is important and can help to prevent your property from being repossessed if you are unable to meet mortgage payments due to a drastic change in circumstances. Also, if you intend to take out a joint mortgage with your child, it will cover against either or both of you being unable to meet payments.

However, you should note that this type of insurance might not be the most appropriate for your needs as it can be expensive and, depending on your circumstances, there might be more suitable alternative sources of finance available such as a redundancy payment or sickness pay. Before taking out this type of insurance, you should consider the following points:

- Pre-existing medical conditions, stress or back problems may not be covered.

- If you were to become unemployed, would you receive a redundancy payment? This could be substantial and would mean that the unemployment part of the policy would not be necessary.

- If you had to leave your job due to illness, would you receive statutory sick pay? Many public sector workers are able to receive a substantial proportion of their salary in sick pay, so this would make the sickness part of the policy unnecessary.

- Check your other insurance policies, such as life insurance or critical illness cover, as some will offer the same cover, or similar cover, which means that you would not need both policies.

- If you are self-employed, you will need to check whether you are covered. Also, you will need to have worked continuously with the same company on a permanent contract for a period of at least 12 months to be eligible to claim on the unemployed part of the policy.

- Find out the length of time over which you would receive payments if you claimed on this insurance. You may find that if the policy only pays for a certain time your savings could cover this period and you might be better adding to your savings rather than paying an expensive premium for insurance that you might never claim.

- What is the maximum payout amount? Would this be sufficient to cover your outgoings?

Although you should not rely on rental income for your investment property to cover you in unforeseen circumstances, you can take this into account when deciding whether you need this type of insurance. For example, even if you were sick or incapacitated, would your rental income cover payments to a property management company so that you would not need to manage or maintain the property yourself? A leaflet called *A Guide to Payment Protection Insurance* is available from the Association of British Insurers' website (www.abi.org.uk).

Critical illness insurance

Critical illness insurance pays out a tax-free lump sum if you are diagnosed with a critical illness, whether or not you survive that illness. This can help you to pay off mortgage debt and reduce the stress associated with meeting payments on your investment property when you are ill. However, this type of cover only pays out once, so you will need to make sure that the amount paid out is enough to cover your debts or that you have other cover in place. Some illnesses may not be covered in your plan, or your premium will be raised if you want certain conditions to be covered. Also, you may not be able to obtain cover for certain pre-existing conditions or if you have received medical treatment for other illnesses, so you must check the small print before making arrangements.

In certain circumstances your insurer may impose other conditions when you make your application. This may be due to your own medical history or that of your family. In these situations the premium that you had been quoted may be increased, so you should check that you are happy with this increased amount and that you understand the conditions before you sign. It is possible to cancel within 30 days of taking out the policy and get back your money if you have not made a claim.

Landlord's insurance

This type of insurance is also known as 'buy-to-let' insurance and covers properties that are let to tenants. This insurance protects you against losing your capital investment and can also help to protect the income that you receive from your tenants. Although policies vary, in general this type of insurance should cover the following:

- property damage;
- buildings;
- contents of communal areas;
- money;
- assault;
- loss of rent and alternative accommodation expenses;
- property owner's liability;
- landlord's contents;
- employer's liability;
- landlord's insurance legal protection.

In most cases you can pick and choose the type of cover that you require, reducing your premium accordingly. There are many competitive policies available, so shop around for the best deal. If you join a local landlord's group, speak to other landlords about the best insurance deals in the area.

On some types of property you will find it very difficult to obtain landlord's insurance, so you need to take this into account when buying a property for letting purposes. Typically this includes flats above premises that are used for the cooking trade, such as fish and chip shops; properties that have been affected by subsidence or flood; and properties in a poor state of repair, or unfit for habitation.

Holiday home insurance

Some insurance companies will arrange special insurance for holiday homes. However, you will need to shop around for the most appropriate policy for your needs as some policies have restrictions on cover, such as you must check the property weekly and not leave it uninhabited for more than 30 days at a time. If you intend to let your holiday home, you will need to find an appropriate policy and make sure that it includes the following:

- buildings;
- employer's liability insurance;
- public liability insurance;
- accidental damage to contents;
- accidental damage caused by holidaymakers;
- loss of pre-booked rental income;
- cost of alternative accommodation;
- insurance for swimming pools, including public liability for use of the pool by guests, if relevant;
- legal expenses protection.

Again, this type of insurance will not be offered on certain types of holiday home, so you will need to take this into account when making your purchasing decisions. Typically this will include 'chalet' type constructions with flat or felt roofs, properties with tin, steel or metal roofs, thatched holiday homes and properties that are left permanently unoccupied.

Guarantee Protection Insurance

Guarantee Protection Insurance (GPI) was set up to cover the type of work on your property that was not covered by other insurance companies, such as rising damp, wet rot, dry rot, woodworm and failing wall ties, which hold cavity walls together. Now it has been expanded to cover such items as structural waterproofing, double glazing and conservatories. The insurance is provided for a one-off payment and can cover ten or 20 years, depending on the type of work carried out. Each piece of work will need to be insured separately and will be covered even if the manufacturer or installer goes out of business.

GPI provides specialist insurance cover which relates to the property rather than the owner. If you decide to sell your property, the insurance is transferred automatically free of charge to the new owners. This is useful for property investors who intend to sell their property at a later date as it provides potential purchasers with peace of mind and can be a useful addition to the Home Information Pack. Therefore, all insurance certificates should be stored safely until you decide to dispose of the property. More information about GPI, along with a list of approved contractors, can be obtained from their website (www.gptprotection.co.uk).

Knowing when and how to sell

Finding the right time to sell your property will depend on a number of factors, which include the following:

- your investment plans for your child;
- the performance of the housing market, including short-term fluctuations;
- your financial circumstances;
- tax liability and the relief and exemptions available;
- your child's age.

Chapter 1 offered advice about monitoring the housing market and being able to predict future trends and prospects, especially in terms of short- and long-term fluctuations. If you do this successfully, you will know when the right time to sell your property is. Even if you had planned to sell the property when your child reached a significant age, you must make sure that it is prudent to do so at this time to maximise your profit. It is important not to stick rigidly to the 'significant age' criterion if there is a slump in the housing market at that time.

You should note that professional investors 'de-risk' investments as they approach maturity. This is a process where the total risk to the investment is identified, prioritised and managed appropriately. In terms of your property investment this would involve a careful assessment of market conditions prior to the expected disposal date. This assessment might indicate that it is better to sell a property earlier than you had intended if there is a chance that the market will slump just before the date you had originally had in mind to sell. The proceeds can be placed into something more secure, such as a high yield account until you wish to pass the money to your child. Alternatively, some investors choose to wait until the value of their property reaches a pre-defined amount, and once this occurs, they go ahead and sell, again, investing the proceeds until their children are old enough to receive the money.

Making a successful sale

When you decide to sell, you will increase your chances of making a successful sale if you take note of the following points:

- **Understand the market.** Know who you are aiming your property at and make sure that your property appeals to this market, in terms of décor, fittings, fixtures and furnishing. Also, think about the positive points of the neighbourhood and location that will appeal to your intended market, such as good schools, good health services or a high ranking university around the corner.

- **Ask a realistic price.** Visit other properties in the area and speak to estate agents to find out how much properties are sold for and how long they remain on the market. Invite estate agents to value your property – it is advisable to obtain quotations from at least three different agents as some will offer an enhanced valuation in the hope that you will do business with them.

- **Decide on a minimum price that you will accept and add on a negotiation figure.** Buyers are always happier when they think they have negotiated a bargain.

- **'Dress' your property for sale.** Furnished properties sell better than unfurnished properties because it is easier for someone to imagine himself living in the property when it is furnished. Show that each room has a specific function and match this function with your target market. If your property has been let for some time, change soft furnishings and redecorate. Some buyers are less inclined to buy a property that has been let as they think it will not have been well maintained.

- **Finish all small jobs such as touching up paintwork and changing worn carpets.** Make sure taps are not leaking and that there are no unpleasant smells in the property. Air it thoroughly rather than relying on chemical air fresheners. Make sure the property is clean throughout, especially the bathroom, kitchen and windows.

- **Remove all clutter but leave enough in the house to give it a 'lived-in' feel.** Remove unnecessary window dressings to let light into the house. Cut down ivy or other creepers around windows. Potential buyers are always drawn to windows and the view outside, so make sure that this is as pleasant as possible. This may involve tidying land and pathways outside that may not belong to you, so always seek permission first, if you are able to locate the owner.

- **First impressions are extremely important.** Think about how a potential purchaser will approach your property and make sure that it looks good, with a new or painted front door and tidy front garden. If he is arriving by car, remove your car from the driveway and invite him to park on the drive.

- **Think about how you are to show potential purchasers around the property.** Note all the positive points of the property and make sure that you sell these. Prepare answers to questions that may be asked, such as, 'Why are you selling?' 'How long have you lived here?' 'What are the neighbours like?' You should not lie to potential purchasers, but by thinking about questions in advance you will be able to highlight the positive points and avoid the more negative aspects.

Using estate agents

When you ask for a valuation from an estate agent he will give you an estimate of how much he thinks your property is worth. He is not fully trained surveyor and will not provide an accurate valuation, so you should check whether you are happy with his valuation and make sure that it matches how much you think the property is worth. Some estate agents may suggest a lower price in order to get a quick sale, whereas others might suggest a higher price in the hope that you will choose to do business with them (see below).

If you decide to use estate agents, make sure that they are registered with the National Association of Estate Agents (see chapter 8) or the Ombudsman for Estate Agents (www.oea.co.uk), as they have to abide by a Code of Conduct and both organisations have a useful complaints procedure. Estate agents will charge anything from 1.5 to 4 per cent commission, and you should remember to add VAT onto the total commission price. Contracts tend to be of three types:

1   'With sole selling rights', which means that you cannot use the services of another agent and if you sell the property yourself you will still have to pay commission to the estate agent.

2   'Sole agency', which means that the estate agent is entitled to commission if you sell your property to a buyer introduced to you by the estate agent within the period of your contract. You would also have to pay commission if you were to sell your property through another estate agent during this contract period. However, if you were to sell your property through your own efforts you would not have to pay commission because you are not an estate agent.

3   'Multi-agency', which means that you can have several agents working for you but only have to pay commission to the one who secures a sale. However, you will pay more commission with this type of contract.

Avoid contracts that use the term 'ready, willing and able to buy' as this means that the estate agent can charge commission when he introduces someone to your property. This means that you would have to pay commission even if your property is not sold. Before signing a contract make sure that you are clear about the terms and conditions and the costs involved.

Selling the property yourself

You do not have to use an estate agent and today there are a large number of websites that enable you to sell your property cheaply and efficiently, saving an average of £4,100 on estate agent fees, according to Houseweb (www.houseweb.co.uk). When using property websites, find out how much you need to pay, checking whether there is a one-off fee, commission and/or final charges when your property is sold. Choose a website that enables you to display a photograph of your property and find out how long it will advertise your property for. It is best to find a website that will advertise your property until it is sold.

If you decide to sell your property yourself, you can erect a 'for sale' board to advertise your property, but you must comply with the Town and Country Planning (Control of Advertisements) Regulations 1992. In Scotland you must comply with the Town and Country Planning (Control of Advertisements) Regulations 1990. If you are selling a flat within a building, you must make it clear to which unit the board relates. Advice about erecting a 'for sale' board within the regulations can be sought from your local planning authority.

Summary

It is not possible to know exactly what will happen in your life, how your personal circumstances might change, or how the property market and your investment will perform over the years. However, it is possible to protect your property through careful management and maintenance and protect your investment against unforeseen circumstances that can have a negative impact on your plans. This includes taking out insurance to cover changing circumstances, such as illness, injury and unemployment, or insurance to pay off your mortgage and other debts if you should die unexpectedly. You can reduce the IHT liability for your children by making sure that life assurance policies are placed in trust.

Protecting your investment also involves making sure that you are not at the mercy of short-term fluctuations in the market, and that you know how and when to sell your investment property to obtain the best price possible.

Once you have made sure that your property and investment are protected, you need to make sure that your child's inheritance is also protected, especially if you were to die unexpectedly. There are two ways to do this – writing a Will and setting up a trust – both of which enable you to specify how you wish to leave your investment property to your child. Writing a Will is discussed in the following chapter.

CHAPTER 11

Leaving property in your Will

As a property investor you must make sure that you choose the way your money is left to your children after your death. The best way to do this is to ensure that you have a valid and up-to-date Will. The rise in property prices has made homes and second homes valuable assets and you must make sure that your property is distributed to your children in a tax efficient manner in order to maximise your investment. It is important, also, to appoint executors who understand your investment plans and can carry out your wishes effectively and efficiently. If your children are under the age of 18, you will need to appoint guardians to look after them and trustees to look after their inheritance, as they cannot legally own property until they reach the age of 18. Advice about all these issues is offered in this chapter.

Drawing up a Will

It is possible to draw up a Will yourself, using a Will writing pack such as *The Last Will and Testament Kit*, Lawpack. This Kit provides a quick, economical and legally valid way to draw up a Will, providing information about the laws of intestacy and drawing attention to all the important considerations and procedures that are involved in writing a Will. It contains ready-to-use Will forms and a CD from which you can download a wide range of useful documents related to Wills. The information contained within the Kit is valid in England and Wales, Scotland and Northern Ireland.

If you decide to draw up your own Will, it is best to use plain English and avoid legal jargon. You will need to make an inventory of everything you own and decide whether there are specific gifts that you want to leave to family and friends. However, when you are leaving property to your children there are certain circumstances where you should seek advice from a solicitor before you draw up your Will, such as:

- if you share a property with someone who is not your spouse or civil partner;

- if you have a property overseas;

- if you have established a property company or partnership;

- if you are not a British citizen or you do not live in the UK;

- in cases where several family members could make a claim, for example if there are ex-spouses and stepchildren;

- in cases where you need to make financial provision for someone who is not able to care for himself, such as a child with disabilities.

Understanding the costs

If you want help drawing up your Will, then you can use a solicitor or Will writer. A solicitor will typically charge £150–£250 and a Will writer will charge £50–£100. When using a Will writer you must make sure that he is fully qualified, a member of the relevant professional association and that he has Professional Indemnity Insurance cover to protect his clients. Also, some Will writers may try to sell you other products, but don't be persuaded to buy expensive products that you do not need. All solicitors have professional qualifications and are supervised by the Law Society. They will have the necessary insurance and an established complaints procedure if you have any problems. Also, they will be able to offer advice on other aspects of property law which may be of use to your investment and inheritance plans, especially if you have a property company or partnership.

You can find an experienced solicitor in your area by using the Law Society's online directory (www.lawsociety.org.uk). You can find a Will writer in your area by contacting the Society of Will writers (www.thesocietyofwillwriters.co.uk) or the Institute of Professional Will writers (www.ipw.org.uk).

Storing your Will

It is important to let your executors know where your Will is kept so that it can be found easily on your death. If your Will cannot be found, there is a legal presumption that it was destroyed or no longer exists. You shouldn't attach anything to your Will with staples or paper clips as it may appear that items have been attached after your death, or lost since the Will was written. Your executors will find it helpful if you store useful information with your Will. In terms of property investment, this could include the following:

- information about outstanding mortgages on any property that you own, including contact details of lenders;
- relevant documents of all the properties that you own, such as title deeds and tenants' contracts;
- addresses of all properties that you own;
- details of your life assurance policy;
- the name and address of your financial adviser.

Changing your Will

When your circumstances change in a significant way, such as through divorce, birth, death, inheritance or an increase in your property portfolio, you will need to change your Will. You cannot make amendments on your original Will after it has been signed and witnessed and any obvious alterations are assumed to have been made at a later date and so do not form part of the original valid Will.

There are two ways that you can change your Will, first by adding a supplement, known as a 'codicil', and second by producing a new Will. A codicil enables you to make some alterations while leaving the original intact, and you can add as many as you wish. All codicils must be signed and witnessed in the same way as the original, although you don't have to use the same witnesses. However, this is only suitable for minor changes, such as adding a beneficiary or increasing a cash legacy. If changes are major or complex you should write a new Will, which begins with a clause stating that all previous Wills and codicils are revoked. This means that all previous Wills are no longer legally valid and you should make sure that they are destroyed in your presence.

Author's note

As five of us are involved in our property company we felt it was very important to sit down and discuss what we hoped to happen to our investment when we died. For the moment we have agreed to leave each of our shares to the surviving owners of the company, but there is concern about how this will affect the inheritance of the children from each family.

We are currently in discussion about setting up a trust to leave the property to our children (see chapter 12). However, a major stumbling block is that one of our brothers is not happy about using a trust, as he believes tax rules are too complex for our needs. It's not all plain sailing when you are part of a family-run business, and this issue has led to a few heated discussions. As yet, it remains unresolved.

Appointing executors

When you draw up your Will you will need to appoint executors to administer your estate after you die and make sure that your wishes are carried out. The executors collect together all the required information and work out the value of your property. They can also act as trustees if your children are under the age of 18 or if you have decided to leave your property in trust (see chapter 12).

You can choose to appoint your partner, a close friend, a family member or a professional to act as executor. However, a professional will charge a fee, so you can save money for your heirs by appointing a relative or friend. You can choose to appoint your children as executors only if they are over the age of 18. When appointing an executor you must discuss the issue with them to make sure that they are happy and able to carry out this role.

An executor will need to undertake the following:

- Collect together all the relevant information concerning your property, assets and investments.

- Obtain professional valuations for property and valuables.

- List the value of all your assets, property and investments.

- Make sure your funeral takes place according to your wishes and that all funeral expenses are paid.

- Find out about outstanding bills and debts.

- Find out about pension entitlement and any other monies that may be due, such as life insurance policies. Certain pensions may pay death benefits or provide a pension for your spouse, civil partner or children.

- Work out how much tax is due and fill in the appropriate forms. Pay tax within the set time limit and receive confirmation that all tax has been paid and no further tax is due.

- Complete and submit Probate Registry forms.

- Call in all assets.

- Pay all debts.

- Transfer gifts to beneficiaries, according to your wishes.

- Draw up clear accounts to give to the beneficiaries.

You can make the work of your executor easier by ensuring that you keep easily accessible records of all your assets, property and investments, including the latest valuations, mortgage information and up-to-date contact details of relevant organisations.

Appointing guardians

As a parent, one of the most important reasons for writing a Will is so that you can appoint guardians to look after your children. If you do not do this, you have no control over who looks after them, should anything happen to you and your spouse/partner. In these circumstances the courts will appoint a guardian on your behalf and this may not be someone that you would have chosen. Where parents are married it is usual for such appointments to take effect on the death of the second parent. In cases where parents are unmarried, divorced or separated, special rules apply and you should seek appropriate advice.

When children are young it may be advisable to appoint close, trusted family members as guardians. However, if children are older you may find it more appropriate to appoint close friends, especially if they have children that are good friends with your children. Substitute guardians can be appointed to cover against changes in circumstances. All appointments must be discussed with potential guardians to make sure that they are happy and able to take on the role.

The role of the guardians is to bring up your children in a manner with which you would agree. You can include a letter with your Will that outlines your wishes for their upbringing, but it is advisable not to be too rigid or dictate to your guardians as this will make their job much harder and could lead to resentment, either from your children or from the guardians.

In your Will you should make financial provision for your children. If your children are under the age of 18 and are to benefit from your estate, you should name them as the beneficiaries, although they will not be able to legally own land or buildings until they reach the age of 18. Responsibility for financial control should be passed to a trustee, rather than to your nominated guardians, as this will provide an extra safeguard against your child's inheritance being squandered. Information about appointing trustees is provided in chapter 12.

Covering against divorce or separation

Although divorce does not automatically invalidate your Will, any gifts that you have made to your ex-spouse will be cancelled and he will not be able to act as an executor. His share will be divided between the other beneficiaries or otherwise disposed of according to instructions in the Will. If your separation has been amicable and you want to leave something to your ex-spouse, you can do so by making specific mention of this in your Will.

After divorce your ex-spouse's children or other family members will still inherit if you have made provision for them in your Will. The best course of action is to rewrite your Will if you separate or divorce so that you can leave your estate to the people that you choose. However, you should note that the Inheritance (Provision for Family and Dependants) Act 1975, and the Inheritance (Provision for Family and Dependants) Order (Northern Ireland) 1979, entitles certain people to apply to court for 'reasonable financial provision', from your estate, even if you have made a Will. Therefore you will need to protect against this happening. Advice for doing so is provided in chapter 2.

In 1995, the government passed a new measure called the Law Reform Succession Act 1995, which amended the 1975 Inheritance Act. This amendment means that if you are not married or in a civil partnership you can still seek financial provision from your partner if he has died without making a Will. However, this amendment also enables others, such as separated spouses or dependent children from another marriage, to make financial claims on your estate. Most separations and divorces are not amicable and you may not wish a previous partner to receive anything from your estate. To prevent this from happening you must make sure that you write a Will and include a written statement as to why a particular person should not receive financial help from your estate. More information about this procedure is provided in chapter 2.

Another option if you are getting divorced is to set up a trust that enables you to make sure that assets go only to children of your marriage, so that any new partner or subsequent children of your ex-spouse cannot benefit from your assets (see chapter 12).

Safeguarding your property investment

Drawing up a Will is the best way to make sure that your property investment is left to your children. If you have several properties, or you have established a property company or partnership, you should seek specialist advice about drawing up a Will. This is of particular importance if you have set up the company or partnership with someone who is not your spouse or civil partner. Also, if you own property jointly with someone else you need to find out whether it is held as 'joint tenants' or as 'tenants in common'. Any land or property that you own as a joint tenant cannot be left in your Will and will pass to your co-owner unless you sever the joint tenancy (see chapter 2). Joint tenancies have to be severed during your lifetime and cannot be severed in your Will.

If you own a foreign property (Scotland, Northern Ireland and Ireland), you may need to make a Will in that foreign country. You will need to seek specialist local advice to make sure that this is done correctly so that your child's inheritance is protected.

Deed of Variation

Some families find that one partner dies before adequate estate planning has taken place, and that his Will does not account for changes in financial and family circumstances. As he has not planned carefully his children discover that there is a large IHT bill to pay when the surviving spouse dies. In these circumstances it is possible to apply for a 'Deed of Variation', which enables the surviving spouse effectively to rewrite the Will of the spouse who has died. This Deed of Variation can be used to divert money elsewhere, either directly to the children, or, if the surviving spouse needs the money, into a discretionary trust (see chapter 12).

A Deed of Variation can also be used to vary the statutory intestacy rules in cases where there is no Will (see chapter 2). This may be useful in cases, for example, where someone is in line to receive a gift from the estate, but he does not want or need the gift and feel that it should go to someone else who is further down the line according to the laws of intestacy.

The Deed of Variation must be put into effect within two years of the first death and all main beneficiaries must agree to the changes in the Will. The variation must be made in writing and all the relevant beneficiaries must sign the document. A variation cannot be made in return for any payment of money or assets. Deeds of Variation can be complex and if you find that you need to follow this route you should seek appropriate professional advice.

Summary

As a parent and property investor you must write a Will so that you can choose how to leave your property and assets to your children after your death. For a Will to be valid it must be produced in writing and witnessed by two people who are not beneficiaries under your Will. It must be stored in a safe place with other documents that will be useful to the executors. Your executors can be your children, if they are over the age of 18. You will need to appoint guardians for your children if they are under the age of 18 and you should discuss this role with potential guardians before they are nominated.

As we have seen previously, if your children are under the age of 18 they cannot legally own land or buildings, so you will need to think about how you would like them to inherit their property. The most common way to do this is by setting up a trust. These issues are discussed in the following chapter.

A useful leaflet called *Why Make a Will?* can be downloaded from the STEP website (details in chapter 12). This leaflet provides a brief explanation of the importance of making a Will and is updated annually, to take into account any changes as a result of the UK Budget. The information supplied relates to England and Wales.

CHAPTER 12

Leaving property in trust

Trusts are a useful way to leave property and assets to your children, especially if they are under the age of 18. A trust can be set up in your lifetime or on your death. A trust is an obligation binding a person, known as the trustee, to deal with property in a specific way for the benefit of another person, known as the beneficiary. The person who passes the property into trust is known as the settlor, which is why some trusts are called settlements. You can put practically any kind of asset into a trust, including cash, stocks, bonds, insurance policies, land, property and artwork. When a trust is set up, the trustees become the legal owners of the property and assets. However, if you are putting property into trust for your children and you also have a spouse to consider then the surviving spouse can still live in a property and enjoy the assets that are owned by a trust for their lifetime. In this case the surviving spouse is known as the 'life tenant' (see below).

There are different types of trust available and the type that you choose to set up depends on a number of factors, such as the age of your children, the value and type of investment property, the age at which you wish your children to inherit and how much control you want the trustees to have over the trust and your property. Also, the type of trust that you choose depends on whether you wish the trust to generate an income, such as when a property is placed in trust and then it is let to tenants to generate a rental income, or a trust to generate a pool of cash when you die, such as a trust funded by a life insurance policy (see chapter 10).

This chapter provides an introduction to the different types of trust, discussing how they might be suitable for your family circumstances and highlighting the tax implications of each. It also illustrates how to set up and manage a trust. However, trust law can be complex and if you are thinking about following this route it may be prudent to seek independent professional advice.

Setting up a trust

As we have seen above, if you are thinking about setting up a trust you should seek the advice of a solicitor or a trust specialist. You can find a solicitor who specialises in trust law from the Law Society website (www.lawsociety.org.uk) and you can obtain contact details of a specialist trust adviser by contacting the Society of Trust and Estate Practitioners (STEP) (www.step.org). These people will be able to discuss your options, offer advice about the most appropriate trust for your needs and circumstances, and provide all the relevant trust forms.

When you set up a trust a 'written declaration of trust' is completed to provide a permanent record of the exact terms of the trust. This is a document that identifies the trust property, names the beneficiaries or group of beneficiaries and sets out the rules on how the trustees can deal with the property and the distribution of assets. Although no particular form or style is required, the words used must be sufficiently clear to show an intention to create a trust. It is best, therefore, to seek legal advice or use an appropriate trust form supplied by your adviser or solicitor. The type of form and wording used will depend on the type of trust you intend to set up; for example, there are trust forms with fixed wording (e.g. suitable for bare trusts) where named beneficiaries cannot be changed, and trust forms that are more flexible (e.g. suitable for discretionary trusts) that enable trustees to choose who should benefit. More information about these different types of trust is provided below.

Putting a property into trust

The method that is used to put property (e.g. your home or an investment property) into trust depends on whether you intend to set up a trust on your death or during your lifetime. Any change of ownership of property must normally be in writing so, if you intend to set up the trust on your death the relevant clauses, or the 'written declaration of trust', must be included in your Will. This will satisfy the requirement for the change of ownership to be in writing. Your personal representatives, once they are satisfied that your beneficiaries are entitled to the property, will assent to the transfer and your beneficiaries become the owner, even if they do not immediately take possession of the property.

If you want to transfer property into a trust that you are setting up during your lifetime, the Settled Land Act 1925 requires two documents:

1   a 'vesting deed' conveying the land to the life tenant (which could be the surviving spouse) or statutory owner (usually the trustees) as legal owner;

2   a 'trust instrument', or written declaration of trust, setting out beneficial interests, appointing the trustees and declaring the trusts.

Both of these documents can be drawn up by your solicitor. These documents enable the trustees to prove their ownership of the property, while not divulging details of the beneficiaries. This is sometimes referred to as the 'curtain principle'.

Choosing trustees

When you set up a trust you will need to decide who is to become a trustee. This can be you, your spouse, a trusted friend or relative, or a professional, such as a solicitor, accountant, or a trust and estate practitioner. Also, most high street banks have related trust fund companies that have been set up for the specific purpose of administering trust funds. Although you will have to pay for the services of a professional or a trust fund company, it is advisable to do this if you don't have the required financial and organisational skills to manage the trust yourself. A professional can also save money in the long run by knowing about tax relief.

A total of four trustees can be appointed and it is advisable that you have at least two trustees. Minors and those 'of unsound mind' (i.e. not of sound mind, memory or understanding) cannot be trustees and you should make sure that you choose trustees who are likely to act in accordance with your wishes and are able to make a long-term commitment. If you are setting up a trust in your lifetime, you should consider becoming a trustee yourself as you can have a say in how the trust is administered. Indeed, many life assurance companies will automatically appoint you as a trustee if you choose to place your life assurance policy in trust (see chapter 10).

Your trustees will need to undertake the following duties:

- invest trust monies as they think fit;

- administer the trust in accordance with the laws that govern trusts;

- respond to any changes in taxation or legislation that may affect the trust;

- respond to any changes in family circumstances that may affect the trust.

Choosing the beneficiaries

When setting up a trust you will also need to think about your beneficiaries (i.e. any individual, charity or legitimate organisation) and how you would like to divide your assets between them. This will involve a careful assessment of all your assets and their value, which will include any property that you have bought for investment purposes. Also, you will need to decide whether your beneficiaries should have an absolute 'fixed' interest in the trust property, such as in a bare trust where they are specifically named, or whether you want your beneficiaries to be chosen at the discretion of your trustees. In this case you will need to provide a list of all potential beneficiaries from which the trustees can choose at their discretion. For example, you may intend to leave some of your estate to your grandchildren and any grandchildren that have not yet been born, whom you cannot yet name. In this case, 'my grandchildren and future grandchildren' will suffice because the trustees understand your wishes and can use their discretion when distributing assets to grandchildren in the future.

Managing a trust

When managing your trust, the trustees must inform HM Revenue & Customs as soon as it has been created if it is liable to tax on income or gains. They can do this by completing the HM Revenue & Customs form 41G (Trust) that can be downloaded from their website (www.hmrc.gov.uk). A sample form is provided in Appendix 6 for your information.

Trustees must undertake the following duties when managing a trust:

- Notify HM Revenue & Customs that tax is due. This must be done within six months of the due date, if they have not received a tax return.

- Keep records of the income and capital gains of the trust.

- Complete and send back tax returns, if relevant.

- Pay any tax that is due on the income or capital gains of the trust.

- Supply certificates or vouchers to the beneficiaries to show how much income they have received from the trust and how much tax has been deducted.

When a trust ceases to exist HM Revenue & Customs will need to be notified and the trustees will need to make provision for any tax that is due. They will also need to consider whether there is any CGT liability in the ending of the trust.

Ensuring your funds are protected

The best way to ensure that your funds are protected is to seek the advice of an experienced professional. If you use a member of a professional association, you should be covered against professional negligence if things go wrong.

You also need to make sure that you appoint trusted and competent trustees. Trustees are the legal owners of the trust property and as such are legally bound to look after the property of the trust. It is imperative that you discuss your wishes, or leave clear instructions, with your trustees so that they understand fully what you are trying to do with your investment. This is one reason why it may be preferable to become one of the trustees yourself. You also need to make sure that your trust is protected by nominating someone else to take over if anything should happen to you. You should be careful not to appoint people where there could be conflicting financial interests, such as a family member who will benefit from the trust upon the death of the life tenant.

Leaving a property in trust to your minor child or children

As we have seen previously, children under the age of 18 cannot legally own land or buildings. If your children are under the age of 18 when you die and you have not made a Will or set up a trust, your property will be held in trust automatically for them. This is called a 'statutory trust' and each child receives a share of the assets on reaching the age of 18 or on marriage if that is earlier. These types of trust can also be known as 'trusts for sale', which means that trustees have the power to sell the property, but also the discretion to postpone the sale. They can defer the sale for as long as they see fit and any money from the sale must be reinvested for the benefit of the beneficiaries. The trustees are appointed by the court under the rules of intestacy if you have not made a Will. These rules do not apply to Scotland and Northern Ireland.

If you want to have more control over what happens to your home or investment property, there are different types of trust available that enable you to manage and maintain your property according to your wishes, rather than according to the rules of intestacy. You should give some thought to this as it will help to protect your children's inheritance after your death and make sure that the trust is run according to your wishes. You can also use a trust to stop your children wasting their inheritance when they get older or you can use a trust to protect their inheritance against you and your spouse separating, divorcing or remarrying in the future.

There are various types of trust and these are described below. There are different tax implications, depending on the type of trust that you choose and the manner in which you wish your children to inherit. For example, you can choose to leave your property in a discretionary trust, which protects against your child squandering a significant amount of capital when he reaches the age of 18 (see below). If there was only a statutory trust, your child would inherit all of his share at the age of 18, whether or not he was responsible enough to handle this amount of money.

However, if you choose the discretionary trust option there are different rates of IHT payable, depending on whether you set up the trust during your life or on your death. Because of these different rates, you can reduce the IHT bill for your children if you set it up during your lifetime, although there will be an IHT charge every ten years on the trust. This is called a 'periodic charge' and is described below. It is possible to avoid paying this charge by setting up a 'bereaved minor's trust' rather than a discretionary trust (see below). If you choose the bereaved minor's trust option the trust would have to be created on your death for the benefit of your minor child and the trust assets would have to be transferred to your child when he reaches the age of 18. This option would not be suitable if you feel that your child could not be trusted to deal with a significant inheritance at this age.

If you choose to set up a trust, CGT can be quite hefty, but can be significantly reduced with careful planning. For example, if you buy a property and transfer it to a trust at the same time, there would be no gain, whereas if you buy a property and then dispose of it to a trust at a later date there would be CGT of 18 per cent to pay on any gains. Also, your child (or the trustees, depending on the type of trust) would have to pay CGT when he disposes of the property.

Leaving property to a disabled child

If you have a disabled child, a key advantage to leaving your home in a discretionary trust after you die is that property put into the trust does not count as an asset for the purposes of the child's benefit calculations. Also, because the property is put into a discretionary trust it does not belong to your child. This means that it cannot be subject to a legal charge by a local authority who may seek to recover the costs of providing care, which could occur if at some point after the death of you and your spouse your disabled child is put into residential care or needs other support from the local authority. You should note that a home placed in a discretionary trust is also protected against a claim for care home fees for the surviving spouse because it is owned by the trust and not by the surviving spouse.

Knowing about the different types of trust

There are various types of trust available to you, as a parent. However, you should note that your family circumstances and your personal wants and needs have a huge influence on the type of trust that is the most suitable, so it may be prudent to seek independent advice tailor-made to your specific needs. A summary of the relevant trusts is provided below.

Discretionary trusts

A discretionary trust is one of the more common types of trusts and tends to be popular because of its flexibility. This type of trust tends to be used by families to make long-term financial provision for their children. It is called a 'discretionary' trust because it enables you to leave important decisions about the running and management of the trust to the discretion of the trustees. This is because funds put into a discretionary trust do not belong to the beneficiaries but belong instead to the trust.

This type of trust is useful if you are undecided about how much of your estate (whether money or property) you would like to leave to your children or if you think that you might want to change your beneficiaries in the future. For example, you could state that while your spouse is alive the capital of the discretionary fund should not be distributed. When your spouse dies the funds should be distributed absolutely to your children who attain the age of 25 in equal shares. However, you can instruct the trustees to distribute the fund on an unequal basis if there were substantial differences in the financial circumstances of your children, a health-related need which required substantial funds, or some other exceptional matter that should occur in the future. Decisions on these matters would be left to the discretion of the trustees, which is useful because none of us can predict what will happen in the future.

As a parent you can use this type of trust to protect your child's inheritance from being spent unwisely when he is not mature enough to handle the money. However, you can make sure that he receives a right to the capital at some time in the future, perhaps when he is settled into his working life and needs the money to buy a house, for example. You can do this by leaving clear instructions to the trustees on your written declaration of trust (see above). Discretionary trusts also enable you to protect your assets against claims that could be made by an ex-spouse's future partner and children.

Discretionary trusts and tax

Your investment property can be placed into a discretionary trust during your lifetime and if you choose to do this at the time you buy the property you should be able to avoid paying CGT on the disposal into the trust because there are no gains, although your children may be liable to CGT when they receive capital from the trust (see below). The date that they receive the capital will be according to your wishes and could be at the discretion of the trustees; for example, it could be when they reach a specified age, or on the death of your spouse.

If you place your investment property into trust during your lifetime, there is an immediate charge to IHT of 20 per cent, with a further charge of up to 20 per cent on death if you die within seven years and depending on the amount of tax that has already been paid (see below). If the property is placed into trust on your death, there is a charge of 40 per cent. However, you should note that this is only charged on assets that are valued over the IHT threshold. Therefore, when a trust is set up there will be no IHT payable if the amount is below this threshold.

Every ten years the property in the trust is valued and any amount over the IHT threshold is subject to an IHT 'periodic charge', with a maximum charge on any one ten-year-anniversary of 6 per cent of the value of the trust fund. (The calculation for the periodic charge works on the assumption that a generation is about 33 years, so it is assumed that the 20 per cent immediate charge, and subsequent periodic charges, should equate to the 40 per cent IHT that would be chargeable on death for property that has not been placed in trust. In making this assumption it is presumed that a trust will be wound up within one generation of the family because most parents are leaving their assets to their children with this type of trust. This rule was brought in to try to stop people avoiding the 40 per cent IHT charge through setting up a discretionary trust.)

If you decide to sell the property and distribute capital before this 'periodic charge', or you try to alter the trust to avoid this payment, you will, in most cases, be subject to an exit charge. This charge is variable and is based on the time the property has been in the discretionary trust since a periodic charge last arose. You will need to work out whether it is better for you financially to pay an exit charge or a periodic charge, and advice should be sought if in doubt.

If you choose to set up this type of trust during your lifetime, the IHT liability for your children will be reduced because you have already paid 20 per cent IHT. However, you should note that your children will have to pay Income Tax on any rental income that they receive from the property that has been placed in a discretionary trust. The income they receive will be net of 40 per cent tax, but your children can claim back any overpaid tax. They may also have to pay CGT but this will depend on the gains on your property and the amount of CGT exemption when they inherit.

Accumulation and maintenance (A&M) trusts

Accumulation and maintenance trusts (A&M) are a special type of discretionary trust that used to be popular because they enjoyed significant tax advantages. However, recent changes to tax rules have led to a decrease in popularity.

If you want to leave your property to your children but do not want them to gain control when they reach 18, you could set up an A&M trust. In England and Wales, the beneficiary normally becomes entitled to the income from the property held in the trust when he reaches the age of 18. In Scotland there is no equivalent entitlement. With this type of trust the trustees can decide whether or not your children receive any capital, usually up until they are aged 25 although even after that age they may decide to hold back the capital. A&M trusts therefore enable you to delay paying capital to your children until they are more able to control their finances, although they will be able to receive income from the trust.

However, capital (that may have accrued from rental income on the property) can be released, at the trustees' discretion, if it is needed to help your children financially.

A&M trusts and tax

Changes that were introduced in March 2006 mean that A&M trusts are now charged IHT on creation. However, the periodic charge of 6 per cent every ten years can be avoided if the trust was created on your death for the benefit of your minor child (under the age of 18) and the trust assets and any accumulated income are passed outright to your children with no conditions attached, when your child reaches the age of 18 (see 'bereaved minor's trust', below). You would have to be happy that your children could manage the property and any capital at the age of 18 if you choose this option.

When an A&M trust is wound up, CGT is payable by the trustees on any gain in the value of the assets being passed to your children above the trust CGT allowance, which is currently £4,800 (2008/09 levels). This amount is half the amount allowed to individuals. After that, your children pay tax on any income or gains in the usual way.

A bereaved minor's trust

A bereaved minor's trust is a trust that is created under a Will and can only be set up by parents for their minor children, who are named specifically in the written declaration of trust. This type of trust cannot be set up by grandparents or other relatives. It has a simple structure that enables your children to receive their inheritance outright at the age of 18. The trustees retain discretion over the use of the income and capital for the benefit of your child until he reaches this age.

A bereaved minor's trust and tax

There are no IHT charges, either during the life of the bereaved minor's trust (i.e. while your children are under 18) or when your children receive their share on reaching the age of 18. Trustees pay CGT when they sell trust assets or pass them to your children.

An age 18 to 25 trust

This is similar to a bereaved minor's trust in that it is created by parents under a Will for minor children. With this type of trust the trustees retain discretion over the use of the income and capital for the benefit of a child until he reaches at least 21, and in many cases depending on the age of the child, until he reaches 25. The formula for working out how much IHT is payable at this time is complex and professional advice should be sought. Trustees pay CGT when they sell trust assets or pass them to your children.

An age 18 to 25 trust and tax

Under an age 18 to 25 trust there is no IHT charge until the child reaches 18, but there is an IHT exit charge payable when he becomes absolutely entitled to the property in the trust (the capital) between the ages of 18 and 25. The formula for working out how much IHT is payable at this time is complex and professional advice should be sought. Trustees pay CGT when they sell trust assets or pass them to your children.

Bare trusts

If you wish to leave your property to your minor children, and you wish to avoid the more complex types of trust, you could set up a bare trust. These can also be known as 'simple trusts' and they are relatively easy to establish. With this type of trust you, as the parents, are the legal owners of the property, while your children become the beneficial owners. This means that the property is held for the benefit of your children, even though you are the legal owner of the property. Once your children turn 18 they can put the property into their own legal ownership, so you would have to be comfortable with this before following this route. Also, you cannot vary the beneficiaries with this type of trust.

Bare trusts and tax

With a bare trust Income Tax and CGT are charged to the beneficiary. However, there should be less CGT to pay once your children's exempt amount is taken into account. IHT will not be charged on your estate because your children are the beneficial owners.

Interest in possession trusts

If you have minor children, you may want to leave your investment property in trust for them, but you may also want to make sure that your spouse has somewhere to live until he dies. In this case an interest in possession trust may be suitable for your needs. These are sometimes referred to as 'life interest trusts', although technically a life interest trust is where an interest in possession ends at the end of the beneficiary's life, whereas an interest in possession trust can end at any specified time.

These trusts enable you to set up a trust that pays an income to your spouse (the life tenant), or enables him to live in your property. At the end of a specified period, which can be upon his death, a pre-determined date or another date decided upon by the trustees, their life interest comes to an end. At this point your children become entitled to trust assets. If your children are under the age of 18 when your spouse dies, the property will be held in trust until they turn 18. These trusts can also be useful in cases of separation and divorce. For example, a divorcee may want his second wife to benefit from an income and live in the family home, but then all assets and the home go to the children of the first marriage on the second wife's death.

Interest in possession trusts and tax

For IHT purposes the life tenant is treated as owning the underlying assets so if your spouse dies while he is a life tenant, the value of the property will be added to his estate for IHT purposes. This means that your children will have an IHT liability if the surviving spouse should die while he is a life tenant. The life tenant is also responsible for meeting any IHT that may be due on the deceased's assets in which he, as life tenant, has an interest in possession (bearing in mind that anything you give to your spouse is exempt from IHT). In terms of CGT, where you have several children entitled to an interest in land, the transfer of which depends on their reaching a certain age, the transfer for CGT purposes occurs when your youngest child reaches the required age.

Author's note

My accountant brother does not like trusts. He thinks they are 'over-complicated, unnecessary, time-consuming and a waste of time'. My financial management brother thinks they are a 'necessary evil' and 'very useful when leaving property to your children'. My other brother, when I asked him what he thought of trusts, said 'leave me alone, I've got a room to paint'. I think they are complicated but can be very useful for parents who wish to protect their investment. I hope I've made them easier for you to understand and that you feel confident about making your own decisions regarding trusts and your property investment. Please do obtain professional advice, though, as trusts can be so complicated.

Summary

Setting up a trust is a useful way to leave property to your children, especially if they are under the age of 18. Trusts can be set up during your lifetime or created on your death under the terms of your Will. There are various types of trust and some, such as a bereaved minor's trust and an age 18–25 trust, reduce the IHT liability for your children. Some trusts, such as discretionary trusts, offer greater flexibility and enable you to leave important decisions to the discretion of your trustees.

If you create a trust during your lifetime and become a trustee yourself, you can make sure that your wishes are carried out and that your children inherit your property in the way that you intend. However, trust rules and regulations can be complex, so you should seek professional independent advice if you are in any doubt.

A useful leaflet called *Why Make a Trust?* can be downloaded from the STEP website (details above). This leaflet provides a brief explanation of the benefit of making a trust, along with some frequently asked questions regarding trusts. It is updated annually and takes into account any changes as a result of the UK Budget.

Conclusion

This book has discussed the various types of property investment that may be suitable for you and your children. It has also provided information that is related to this type of investment, such as planning your finances, understanding inheritance rules, writing a Will and setting up a trust. The next part of this book provides a summary of the different options that may be available to you, as a parent hoping to invest in property for your children. This is followed by checklists to help you make decisions about the most appropriate type of property investment for your children and information about the alternative types of investment opportunity that are available to you as parents. I wish you every success with your property investment and hope that your children appreciate and enjoy their inheritance.

CHAPTER 13

Property investment options – summary

This part of the book provides an overview of the options that are available to you as a parent wishing to invest in property for your children. The option you choose depends on the number and age of your children, your family finances, your family circumstances and your investment preferences.

Each option is summarised below, with more information provided in the relevant chapters. The most important point to note, however, is that every family is different and you need to choose the investment strategy that is most suited to your needs and circumstances. If you are unsure about the most appropriate type of investment, you should seek independent financial advice (see chapter 2).

TABLE 9: A SUMMARY OF PROPERTY INVESTMENT OPTIONS

SCENARIO	INVESTMENT OPTION
You have several children, all under the age of 18. You want to retain control over a second property that you have bought until your children reach 18, when you want the property to be sold and	You can choose to buy a property and immediately set up a trust, thus avoiding CGT when you dispose of the property into the trust. You can appoint yourself and a trusted friend as trustees and let the property to tenants, investing the rental income as you see fit, depending on market circumstances. When your last

the proceeds to be shared equally between your children.

child reaches the age of 18 you can sell the property with the proceeds shared equally between the children. An accumulation and maintenance trust or discretionary trust may be suitable for your needs (see chapter 12). CGT will be payable when the property is sold or when your youngest child reaches the required age. Trustees pay CGT when they sell trust assets or pass them to your children. There will be a charge to IHT that you will have to pay when you set up the trust, and you may have to pay periodic charges and an exit charge, depending on the length of time that the property is held in trust and the type of trust that you choose (see chapter 12). Your children will have an IHT liability if you should die within seven years of their receiving their share, but this will be reduced because of the amount of IHT that has already been paid.

You have one child, under the age of 18. You want your child to inherit your home upon your death, but you need to make sure that you or your spouse has somewhere to live until death. You don't want to be caught in the 'gift with reservation of benefit' trap.

You can decide to set up an 'interest in possession' trust. This enables you to specify that you or your spouse live in the property, and that your child inherits the whole property upon the last survivor's death. If your child is below the age of 18 when you both die, the trust will own and manage the property until your child reaches the age of 18 (see chapter 12). For IHT purposes you or your spouse own the underlying assets, which means that the value of the property will be added to the last survivor's estate. CGT may not be payable if the property is your child's main residence (see chapter 5).

You want to buy a property for your child but you can't put it in his name because he is under the age of 18. However, you've heard that it's more tax efficient to put the property in the child's name.

While it is true that a minor child cannot legally own property or land, it is possible to set up a bare trust that enables you, as the parents, to be the legal owners of the property, while your child is the beneficial owner. IHT will not be charged on your estate because your children are the beneficial owners. Also, there would be no CGT to pay because the property would be your child's main residence (see chapter 5). If the property is let, Income Tax is charged to the beneficiary, which may mean that there is less tax to pay if your child is in a lower tax band. However, your child can put the property into his own legal ownership once he reaches the age of 18, so you would need to be happy with this if you choose this option (see chapter 12). Also, you would not be able to vary the beneficiaries with this type of trust.

You are a single parent and have one young child. Although you don't expect to die before your child reaches the age of 18, you want to make sure that your property goes straight to him, if you die early.

You could choose to set up a bereaved minor's trust. This enables you to specify in your Will that the trust is set up after your death, but this will only happen if your child is under the age of 18 when you die. The property is managed and maintained by the trust until your child reaches the age of 18, at which time your child will inherit outright. There is no charge to IHT and the trustees pay CGT when the property passes to your child (see chapters 11 and 12). If you are still alive when your child turns 18, you can rewrite your Will to take account of your changing needs (see chapter 11).

You have several children under the age of 18. You are divorced and your ex-spouse has not remarried. You have several investment properties that you want to leave to your children, but are concerned that your ex-spouse may try to make a claim after you die, which will affect the amount of money that your children could inherit.	You should include a statement in your Will that states why your spouse should not be able to make a claim against your estate (see chapter 2). Another option is to set up a discretionary trust that enables you to make sure that the properties go only to children of your marriage, so that any new partner or subsequent children of your ex-spouse cannot benefit from your assets (see chapter 12).
Your child has reached the age of 18 and is going away to university. You want to buy a property that he can live in while he is studying. You want to do this in the most tax efficient way.	Since your child is 18 the most tax efficient way is to buy a property in your child's name. You can do this by obtaining a guarantor or first-start mortgage as these enable your child to become the sole owner of the property. This option means that your child would not have to pay CGT when he disposes of the property as it is his main residence (see chapter 5). Also, because the property is not in your name, it will not be added to your estate for IHT purposes on your death. However, you should note that you will be responsible for mortgage payments if your child is unable to pay.
Your child cannot afford to buy a house so you want to help him to do so. However, you are unsure how to go about doing this.	There are various options available to you and this will depend on a number of factors, including your spare capital, your present mortgage commitments, your age and the type of agreement that would most suit your child. You could choose to help him by paying the deposit, taking out a joint mortgage or acting as a guarantor

on a mortgage, (for more information see chapter 7). Any gifts you give for a deposit should be within the IHT annual exemption of £3,000, or you will need to survive the gift by seven years if it is above this amount so that it is not added to your estate for IHT purposes (see chapter 4).

Your child is going away to university and you would like to buy somewhere for him to live, but you want to retain control of the property, perhaps keeping it as an investment property once your child has finished university.	If you have the available capital, you can buy a property outright, if market conditions are favourable, or you can choose to take out a mortgage on the property. The property will not be your main residence, so you will have to pay CGT when you come to dispose of it. Also, it will be added to your estate for IHT purposes on your death (see chapter 5). However, you can decide what happens to the property as it is in your name, and you can choose to keep the property to let to tenants after your child leaves university and moves elsewhere.
All your children are over the age of 18. You want to buy a holiday home that is available for all the family when they want to go on holiday, and you want to use it as an investment to leave to your children when you die.	Second mortgages are available for holiday homes, but in today's economic climate you will need to have a large deposit to obtain a better deal. IHT and CGT may be payable by your children when they inherit and when they dispose of the property. Your Will should detail what you wish to happen to the property upon your death to avoid arguments (see chapter 11).
Your child wants to buy a home but cannot afford to do so. You and your spouse are getting older and your current property is too large for your	You can choose to make use of the IHT annual exemptions for both you and your spouse, and, if you did not make use of these in the previous year you can give a total of £12,000 to your child that will be free of IHT. Alternatively, you can

needs, so you are happy to downsize. You want to give the capital to your child, but don't want this to increase his tax liability on your death. You believe your estate to be considerably higher than the current IHT threshold.

choose to give a larger amount as a potentially exempt transfer (PET) and hope that you survive the gift by seven years (see chapter 4). It may be possible to insure your life under a seven-year-term assurance policy to cover against potential IHT liability (see chapter 10).

You think you will die sooner than your spouse. You want to make sure that your children inherit your home, but you also want to make sure that your spouse has somewhere to live until he dies. However, although you understand that he may remarry and perhaps have more children, you only want your children to inherit your property.

You can set up a 'life interest trust' that enables you to provide an income and somewhere for your spouse to live until he dies. You can specify that only your children are to inherit. Alternatively, you can set up a discretionary trust to protect against future claims (see chapter 12).

Your child is getting married and you want to help him to buy a new home as a wedding present. However, you don't want your child to face a high IHT bill if you should die within seven years.

You and your spouse can use your annual exemption to provide a total gift of £6,000, which could rise to £12,000 if you have not used your exemption from the previous year. You can both also make a wedding gift of £5,000 each. This means that you could give your child a total of £22,000 that he could use as a deposit for a house (see chapter 4). These amounts are exempt and will not be added to your estate for IHT purposes.

APPENDIX 1

Property investment checklist

In the following checklist you should try to answer 'yes' to as many relevant questions as possible as this will maximise the return on your investment. If you answer 'no' to any relevant questions, this suggests that you may need to think again about whether it is prudent to invest in property, conduct some more research, raise more money or enhance your existing skills and knowledge. Obviously not all questions will be relevant – please ignore those that are irrelevant to your position.

		YES	NO
1	Are property prices rising in the UK?	–	–
2	Are property prices rising in the area in which you are interested?	–	–
3	Are you and your family in a secure financial position?	–	–
4	Can you weather fluctuations in the property market?	–	–
5	Can you raise enough capital for your investment?	–	–
6	Have you enough money to put aside for a contingency fund?	–	–
7	Have you produced a profit/loss plan?	–	–
8	Have you produced a cash flow forecast?	–	–
9	Are lenders/financial backers happy with your plans?	–	–
10	Have you weighed up the pros and cons of property investment?	–	–
11	Have you weighed up the pros and cons of other investment?	–	–
12	Have you sought expert financial advice?	–	–
13	Have you conducted comprehensive research?	–	–

14 Have you thought about the implications
    for your children?   —   —

15 Do you understand inheritance rules?
                                                    —   —

16 Have you taken action to reduce IHT?
                                                    —   —

17 Do you understand other tax implications?
                                                    —   —

18 Have you taken action to reduce tax liability? —   —

19 Have you undertaken careful estate planning?   —   —

20 Have you written a Will?
                                                    —   —

21 Is your Will easily accessible and stored safely? —   —

22 Have you appointed trusted executors?
                                                    —   —

23 Do your executors understand your
    investment plans?   —   —

24 Have you appointed trusted guardians?
                                                    —   —

25 Do your guardians understand your
    investment plans?   —   —

26 Are your finances protected by taking out
    adequate insurance?   —   —

27 Is your property protected by taking out
    adequate insurance?   —   —

28 Is your child's inheritance protected by
    taking out adequate insurance,
    setting up an appropriate trust and
    writing a Will?   —   —

29 Do you understand what type of insurance
    is required?   —   —

30 Have you protected against divorce and
    separation, perhaps through setting up an
    appropriate trust and by specifying your
    wishes in your Will?   —   —

31 Have you protected against financial claims
    against your estate, perhaps by setting up an
    appropriate trust and by specifying your
    wishes in your Will?   —   —

32 Have you protected against the loss of your spouse/partner, perhaps by setting up an appropriate trust and by specifying your wishes in your Will? _ _

33 Do you have the right motivation for this investment? _ _

34 Do you have the necessary skills and knowledge? _ _

35 Do you have the support of your family? _ _

36 Do you have adequate time available? _ _

37 Are you aware of the legal implications of your investment? _ _

38 Are your children aware of these legal implications? _ _

39 Are you happy that your children will act responsibly? _ _

40 Have you protected your investment against your children acting irresponsibly, perhaps by setting up an appropriate trust? _ _

41 Have you protected your investment against family arguments, perhaps by setting up an appropriate trust and by making provision in your Will? _ _

42 Will your children gain, financially, because of your plans? _ _

43 Are you satisfied that you will make a sound investment? _ _

APPENDIX 2

Buy-to-let investment checklist

If you are intending to buy a property to let to tenants, there are additional questions that you need to ask. If you answer 'no' to any of these questions you may need to conduct some more research or move on to a more appropriate buy-to-let opportunity.

		YES	NO
1	Do you understand the regulations associated with letting property?	—	—
2	Do you understand the rights of tenants?	—	—
3	Do you understand your responsibilities as a landlord?	—	—
4	Would you be able to take tenants to court, if required?	—	—
5	Are there plenty of potential tenants in the area, if relevant?	—	—
6	Will there be demand for rental properties in the area?	—	—
7	Are you sure buy-to-let saturation point hasn't been reached?	—	—
8	Do you know which type of tenants to attract?	—	—
9	Are these people available?	—	—
10	Are they willing to pay the rent you require?	—	—
11	Are they interested in the type of property you are offering?	—	—
12	Have you spoken to other landlords in the area?	—	—
13	If relevant, is there a good local letting agent in the area?	—	—
14	Is there a good property maintenance company in the area?	—	—
15	Are you sure your buy-to-let plans will yield a good return for your investment?	—	—

APPENDIX 3

Property search checklist

In the following checklist you should try to answer 'yes' to as many relevant questions as possible as this will ensure that you choose a suitable property and maximise the return on your investment. If you answer 'no' to any relevant questions, further research may be required or you might need to consider moving on to other properties that might offer a better investment opportunity. Obviously not all questions will be relevant – please ignore those that are irrelevant to your position.

		YES	NO
1	Are you familiar with the location?	–	–
2	Are prices rising in this location?	–	–
3	Are rents rising in the area?	–	–
4	Is this a good location in which to buy?	–	–
5	If relevant, would your children be happy to live in the area?	–	–
6	Would they be safe doing so?	–	–
7	Would you live in this area?	–	–
8	Are estate agents selling aggressively in the area?	–	–
9	Is the property market moving quickly in the area?	–	–
10	Is there evidence of new development?	–	–
11	Are surrounding areas 'desirable'?	–	–
12	Is the local business sector growing?	–	–
13	Are new shops opening in the area?	–	–
14	Are good schools, colleges and/or universities available locally?	–	–
15	Have you viewed the development plans for the area?	–	–

16   Is the area free from unpopular development proposals?

17   Have you viewed the environment agency information?

18   Is the area free from flooding risk?

19   Is the area free from subsidence risk?

20   Is the area free from unfavourable highways development?

21   Is the area free from pollution risk?

22   Is the area free from graffiti and vandalism? (Of course you could consider taking a gamble and investing in a slightly rougher area if it is surrounded by more desirable areas.)

23   Are crime levels falling in the area?

24   Is the area free from boarded up/empty properties?

25   Are there expensive cars parked in driveways?

26   Are neighbouring properties well kept?

27   Is there evidence of community involvement in the area?

28   Is there a Neighbourhood Watch scheme in place?

29   Are there good social and entertainment facilities nearby?

30   Is there a good transport network available?

31   Are there good health facilities nearby?

32   Are there good leisure facilities nearby?

33   Is the area free from flight path/airport disturbance?

34   Is the area free from mobile masts, erected or proposed?

35   Is there plenty of free parking available?

36 Is the area free from restrictions on planning
and development?   _   _

37 Can you access good, reliable builders and
tradespeople?   _   _

38 In your opinion, would the property make a
good investment?   _   _

APPENDIX 4

Property viewing checklist

In the following checklist you should try to answer 'yes' to as many relevant questions as possible as this will ensure that you find a suitable property and maximise the return on your investment. If you answer 'no' to some of the relevant questions, you need to decide whether there might be other properties that are more suitable for your needs. Obviously not all questions will be relevant – please ignore those that are irrelevant to your position.

		YES	NO
1	Do you know why the property is being sold?	_	_
2	Is it being offered at a good price?	_	_
3	Is the vendor willing to negotiate on the price?	_	_
4	Is the property freehold?	_	_.
5	Is the property free from restrictions on development?	_	_
6	Is it free from listed building status?	_	_
7	Is there vacant possession?	_	_
8	Can you be sure the property has never been flooded?	_	_
9	Is the property located more than 1/4 mile from a watercourse (This could be a river, stream, ditch, culvert, dike, sluice or the sea. Some mortgage companies will not offer a mortgage on a property that has flood potential and most insurance companies will require a much higher premium to insure your property if it is within 1/4 mile of water.)	_	_
10	Does it have a damp proof course?	_	_
11	Is the damp proof course free from obstructions?	_	_

12 Is the property free from smells of damp or
damp patches?   _   _

13 Are any flat roofs free from puddles
when it rains?   _   _

14 Is the roof sound and not bowing?   _   _

15 Are gutters and drainpipes free from
cracks and leaks?   _   _

16 Is it free from cracks in the brickwork
or render?   _   _

17 Is it free from problems with subsidence?   _   _

18 Are window frames free from rot?   _   _

19 Do all windows open smoothly?   _   _

20 Is double glazing free from condensation
between panes?   _   _

21 Is woodwork free from rot or woodworm?   _   _

22 Is it free from creaking floorboards?   _   _

23 Has the property been rewired recently?   _   _

24 Is there adequate water pressure?   _   _

25 Does the central heating system work
efficiently?   _   _

26 Are radiators free from corrosion and leaks?   _   _

27 Is the property well insulated?   _   _

28 Is the kitchen well equipped?   _   _

29 Are kitchen units correctly assembled and
do they function well?   _   _

30 Do you know what appliances are included
in the sale?   _   _

31 Do relevant appliances work?   _   _

32 Are curtains and carpets to be included in
the sale?   _   _

33 Do you know what other fixtures and fittings
are included?   _   _

34	Is the property free from boundary disputes?	_	_
35	Is it free from neighbouring eyesores?	_	_
36	Is the property free from problematic neighbours?	_	_
37	Have you met the neighbours?	_	_
38	Have you visited at different times of the day and week?	_	_
39	Is the property free from noise pollution?	_	_
40	Can you obtain a mortgage on the property, if required?	_	_
41	If relevant, would your children be happy to live in the property?	_	_
42	Would their friends be happy to do so?	_	_
43	Is their college/university close by?	_	_
44	Would you be able to sell the property at short notice?	_	_
45	Are you sure that a student area would not deter purchasers?	_	_
46	Have you seen the Home Information Pack (HIP)?	_	_
47	Is a Home Condition Report included in the HIP?	_	_
48	Are the necessary warranties and guarantees included in the HIP?	_	_
49	Are the necessary completion certificates included in the HIP?	_	_
50	Does the property score well on energy efficiency?	_	_
51	Are you sure the HIP is complete and sound?	_	_
52	Do you think the property will make a good investment?	_	_

APPENDIX 5

Alternative investment opportunities

There are other types of investment that you may wish to consider, in addition to investing in property for your child. Some of these are described below. By taking advantage of these different types of investment opportunity you can spread your risk and this will help you to weather fluctuations in the property market (see chapter 1). However, you should note that only financial advisers that are authorised by the FSA are able to give financial advice, so you should contact a professional in your area for advice suited to your circumstances and needs. Comparative tables for various types of investment product can be viewed on the FSA website (www.fsa.gov.uk/tables). You should also note that there are different tax implications, depending on the type of investment that you choose. Some of these implications are discussed at the end of this Appendix.

Child Trust Fund Accounts

If your child was born after 31 August 2002, you will receive a voucher from the state that must be invested on his behalf. You can invest in a savings Child Trust Fund (CTF) account that works like a normal savings account. However, the interest is tax free and money cannot be withdrawn from the account until your child reaches the age of 18. Or you can choose to invest in a stakeholder CTF account. Using this method the money is invested mainly in the stock market, perhaps through unit trusts, but there are controls in place to reduce the amount of risk. Also, there is a limit to the amount of fee that can be charged by the company that manages the investment. A third option is to invest the money in other types of stock market-linked CTF accounts. These do not meet the conditions of the stakeholder account described above and therefore contain a higher element of risk.

The type of account that you choose is your decision and it is possible to choose ethical accounts, or sharia accounts that are based on Islamic moral values. You can top up the account each year and the maximum that can be paid into a CTF account in any year is £1,200 from all people who wish to make a contribution. The start date for contributions each year is your child's birthday and it is not possible to carry forward any unused contribution to the following year. Comprehensive information and advice about CTFs can be obtained from www.childtrustfund.gov.uk.

Children's savings accounts

Some banks and building societies offer savings accounts for children that have higher interest rates than other types of savings account. They may also offer vouchers, tokens or other perks when an account is opened. Accounts with higher interest rates tend to have greater restrictions, such as a limit to the amount that can be withdrawn, or longer periods of notice before cash is withdrawn. When you open an account you should fill in HMRC form R85 as this will ensure that no tax will be deducted from the interest earned on funds in the account.

National Savings and Investments

National Savings and Investments offer a variety of investment opportunities for parents, and some of these are tax free. Their Children's Bonus Bonds enable you to invest from £25 to £3,000 in each issue and provide a guaranteed rate of interest and a bonus every five years. Premium Bonds can be bought by parents for children under the age of 16 and you can invest £100 – £30,000. They provide the opportunity to win tax-free cash prizes every month. Parents can also invest £100 – £15,000 in Index-Linked Savings Certificates that are guaranteed to beat inflation when held for at least a year. Alternatively, you could choose to open an Investment Account for your child. This is a passbook savings account that enables you to invest from £20 to £100,000. More information about all these savings methods can be obtained from www.nsandi.com.

Friendly Society Children's Saving Plans or Baby Bonds

These are available for parents who want a long-term investment for their children, with most types having a minimum term of ten years. The plan is linked to the stock market investment that is held by the company, so the amount your child will receive at the end of the term depends on the performance of the stock market and the company's investment management. Some companies specialise in providing investment products only for children. The bonds are free from Income Tax and CGT but tend to have low maximum investment levels. More information about friendly societies and a list of links to individual websites can be obtained from the Association of Friendly Societies' website (www.afs.org.uk).

Individual Savings Accounts

If you want to have more flexibility and control over the money that you are investing for your child, you can choose to invest in an individual savings account (ISA). The type of ISA that you choose will depend on how much you wish to invest and for how long, so you should seek specialist advice if you wish to follow this route. However, you should note that, if your children are under the age of 15, the ISA will have to be taken out by you in your name as children under this age cannot have an ISA.

Children aged 16 and 17 can have a cash ISA and the subscription limits are the same as for savers who are over 18, currently up to £3,600 in each tax year. If the ISA is in your name, you do not have to pay Income Tax or CGT on the profit earned. However, if you give money to your child (aged 16 or 17) to invest in an ISA in his name, and the total income earned from the investment exceeds £100 in any tax year, it will be treated as part of your income for tax purposes (see below). Note that this is only the case if your children have taken an ISA in their name and you have contributed the capital.

More information about investing in ISAs can be obtained from HMRC (ISA helpline: 0845 604 1701; www.hmrc.gov.uk/isa) or from your financial adviser.

Unit Trusts, Open-Ended Investment Companies or Investment Trust Savings Plans

If you want to save regularly for your child over the long term, some unit trust or investment trust companies enable you to set up a plan for your child. According to the Association of Investment Companies, investing £50 a month in the average investment company over the last 18 years would have resulted in a sum of £29,330 for your children. However, the performance of your investment depends on the performance of the stock market, so you will have to monitor your investment carefully and make sure that the money is accessed at the right time. Set-up costs and annual charges vary considerably, so you should shop around for the best deal. For unbiased, comprehensive information about unit trusts and open-ended investment companies (OEICs), visit www.which.co.uk.

Pension funds

Parents, grandparents or godparents can contribute to a pension fund for children. At the time of writing the maximum amount you can contribute is £240 a month, which is £2,880 a year and therefore falls within the £3,000 annual exemption for IHT purposes. Even though your children may not pay tax they can still claim basic-rate tax relief on gross contributions into a pension of up to £3,600 per tax year. (This is the maximum figure that a non-earner can contribute towards a pension fund and your children, if they are minors, are seen as non-earners, even though it is you who is making the contribution on their behalf.) This means that the fund will be boosted by an extra 20 per cent (for the tax year 2008/09) of every payment that's made.

According to the *Daily Telegraph*'s financial expert, if you were able to invest this amount of money each year from the time your child is born until his 18th birthday, his fund will be worth around £1.8 million at retirement, assuming a growth of 6 per cent a year. If you can't afford this amount, but instead decided to invest your child allowance into a pension fund, it is likely to produce a fund of nearly £45,600 by the time your child reaches the age of 18. This could be a fund of £700,000 on retirement.

With this type of fund you can make sure that the money is tucked away and cannot be accessed by your children until they reach retirement age. There are various types of pension that you can consider, such as low cost FTSE All-Share trackers, stakeholder pensions and self-invested personal pensions (SIPPS). If you wish to follow this route, you should seek specialist advice to find out which type of pension is the most appropriate for your family circumstances. General information and advice about pensions can be obtained from the Pensions Advisory Service (tel: 0845 601 2923; www.pensionsadvisoryservice.org.uk).

Tax implications

It is possible only to give a general guide to the tax implications of your investment decisions. Every family's tax circumstances are different, and you should seek professional advice tailored to your specific needs. This will help you understand the tax implications and make the most of tax relief, exemptions and allowances.

Generally, if you hold an account or make an investment in stocks or bonds (including ISAs) on behalf of your child that generates an income of more than £100 a year, it will be taken as part of your income and you will have to pay Income Tax on the full amount earned. Note that this is a special rule that applies to savings and investments in stocks and shares for children if they are gifts from parents or if the income from all of the gifts from each parent adds up to more than £100 in a year (see chapter 6). Different rules apply for income generated from property investment, depending on who owns the property and whether he is a resident landlord (see chapter 8). This rule applies until your child reaches the age of 18, if he remains unmarried. You should note that the £100 limit only applies to parents and step-parents. Grandparents and other adults who give money to children are not liable to pay the tax if the interest exceeds £100 a year.

You can overcome this problem by investing in a growth fund that has capital appreciation as its aim and doesn't generate an income from dividends. (Put simply, investment funds tend to be of two types – income and growth. An income fund provides investors with earnings from the dividends of the companies that the fund manager had invested in. A growth fund aims to grow the original sum invested by as much as possible, or sometimes by a specified amount.) However, CGT will be payable by your children when they receive the capital if the fund grows above the exempt amount of £9,600 (2008/09). Alternatively, you can invest in tax-free bonds (see above).

Although the IHT position can be complicated, in most cases savings that you hold in your name on behalf of your children while they are under the age of 18 will be added to your estate for IHT purposes.

APPENDIX 6

IHT 200 form

HM Revenue & Customs

Inheritance Tax Account

Fill in this account for the estate of a person who died on or after 18 March 1986.
You should read the related guidance note(s) before filling in this form.
The notes follow the same numbering as this form for ease of reference.

A Write in the name of the Probate Registry, Commissary Court or Sheriff Court District where you will apply for a grant

A1 [   ]   Date of grant [   ]

B Provide the following information about the person who has died

Title B1 [   ]   Surname B2 [   ]

Other name(s) B3 [   ]

Date of birth B4 [/   /   ]   Date of death B5 [/   /   ]

Marital or civil partnership status   Write whichever is appropriate a, b, c or d in the box B6 [   ]
a married or in civil partnership b single c divorced or former civil partner d widowed or surviving civil partner

Last known permanent address
B7 [   ]   Is B7 a care home? B13 Yes [ ] No [ ]

Domicile B14 [   ]

Postcode   Occupation B15 [   ]

Surviving relatives   National insurance number B16 [   ]
Spouse or civil partner B8 [ ]

Brother(s)/sister(s) B9 [ ]   Income tax district B17 [   ]

Parent(s) B10 [ ]   Income tax or self assessment reference B18 [   ]

Number of children B11 [ ]

Number of grandchildren B12 [ ]   Did the deceased grant a power of attorney? B19 Yes [ ] No [ ]

C If you want us to deal directly with a solicitor or other person provide the following information about them

Name and address of firm or person dealing with the estate
C1 [   ]   DX number and town
C2 DX [   ]

Contact name and reference
C3 [   ]

Telephone number
C4 [   ]

Postcode   Fax number
C5 [   ]

IHT 200   www.hmrc.gov.uk/cto   Helpline 0845 30 20 900   HMRC CT 08/06

D **Supplementary pages**

You must answer all of the questions in this section, by ticking the box that applies.

If you answer "Yes" to a question you will need to fill in the supplementary page shown. If you do not have all the supplementary pages you need you can download them from the internet (www.hmrc.gov.uk/cto) or request them from the orderline: e-mail (hmrc.ihtorderline@gtnet.gov.uk) or telephone 0845 30 20 900.

		No	Yes	Page
• The Will	Did the deceased leave a Will?	☐	☐	D1
• Domicile outside the United Kingdom	Was the deceased domiciled outside the UK at the date of death?	☐	☐	D2
• Gifts and other transfers of value	Did the deceased make any gift or any other transfer of value on or after 18 March 1986 (including gifts with reservation and gifts involving previously owned assets)?	☐	☐	D3
• Joint assets	Did the deceased hold any asset(s) in joint names with another person?	☐	☐	D4
• Nominated assets	Did the deceased, at any time during their lifetime, give written instructions (usually called a "nomination") that any asset was to pass to a particular person on their death?	☐	☐	D4
• Assets held in trust	Did the deceased have any right to any benefit from any assets held in trust or in a settlement at the date of death?	☐	☐	D5
• Pensions	Did the deceased have a pension provision for retirement other than the State Pension?	☐	☐	D6
• Stocks and shares	Did the deceased own any stocks or shares?	☐	☐	D7
• Debts due to the estate	Did the deceased lend any money, either on mortgage or by personal loan, that had not been repaid by the date of death?	☐	☐	D8
• Life insurance and annuities	Did the deceased pay any premiums on any life insurance policies or annuities which are payable to either the estate or to someone else or which continue after death?	☐	☐	D9
• Household and personal goods	Complete form D10 in all cases. If the deceased did not own any household goods or personal possessions or they do not have any value, explain the circumstances on form D10.		☐	D10
• Interest in another estate	Did the deceased have a right to a legacy or a share of an estate of someone who died before them, but which they had not received before they died?	☐	☐	D11
• Land, buildings and interests in land	Did the deceased own any land or buildings in the UK?	☐	☐	D12
• Agricultural relief	Are you deducting agricultural relief from the value of any farm or farmland owned by the deceased?	☐	☐	D13
• Business interests	Did the deceased own all or part of a business or were they a partner in a business?	☐	☐	D14
• Business relief	Are you deducting business relief?	☐	☐	D14
• Foreign assets	Did the deceased own any assets outside the UK?	☐	☐	D15
• Debts owed by the estate	Are you claiming a deduction against the estate for any money that the deceased had borrowed from relatives, close friends, or trustees, or other loans, overdrafts or guarantee debts?	☐	☐	D16

E **Domicile in Scotland - entitlement to claim legal rights**

Scottish legal rights entitlement (jus relicti/æ and or legitim) is relevant to this estate?   No ☐   Yes ☐

How many children are   under 18 ☐   18 and over ☐

F **Estate in the UK where tax may not be paid by instalments**

		Open market value at the date of death
• Quoted stocks, shares and investments *(box SS1, form D7)*	F1	£
• UK Government and municipal securities *(box SS2, form D7)*	F2	£
• Unquoted stocks, shares and investments	F3	£
• Traded unquoted stocks and shares	F4	£
• Dividends or interest	F5	£
• Premium Bonds *(including the value of any unclaimed or uncashed prizes)*	F6	£
• National Savings investments *(show details on form D17, or Inventory form C1 in Scotland)*	F7	£
• Bank and building society accounts *(list each account or investment separately on form D17, or Inventory form C1 in Scotland)*	F8	£
• Cash	F9	£
• Debts due to the deceased and secured by mortgage *(box DD1, form D8)*	F10	£
• Other debts due to the deceased *(box DD1, form D8)*	F11	£
• Rents due to the deceased, but unpaid at the date of death *(Include the property itself on form D12)*	F12	£
• Accrued income	F13	£
• Apportioned income	F14	£
• Other income due to the deceased *(box IP4, form D9, box PA1 form D6)*	F15	£
• Life insurance policies *(box IP3, form D9)*	F16	£
• Payments due to the deceased under private medical insurance to cover hospital or health charges incurred before death.	F17	£
• Income tax or capital gains tax repayment	F18	£
• Household and personal goods *(sold, box HG18, form D10)*	F19	£
• Household and personal goods *(unsold, box HG17, form D10)*	F20	£
• Interest in another estate unpaid at the date of death *(box UE1, form D11)*	F21	£
• Interest in expectancy *(reversionary interest)*	F22	£
• Other personal assets in the UK *(show details on form D17, or Inventory form C1 in Scotland)*	F23	£
Total assets *(sum of boxes F1 to F23)*	F24	£

Liabilities, funeral expenses, exemptions and reliefs

- Liabilities incurred by the deceased before the date of death

Name	Description of liability	

Total liabilities *(write in the total of the items listed above)* **F25** £

- Funeral expenses

Total funeral expenses *(write in the total of the items listed above)* **F26** £

Total liabilities and funeral expenses
(box F25 plus box F26. If box F27 is more than box F24 see explanatory notes) **F27** £

Net total of assets less liabilities *(box F24 less box F27)* **F28** £

- Exemptions and reliefs

Total exemptions and reliefs *(write in the total of the items listed above)* **F29** £

Chargeable value of assets in the UK where tax may not be paid by instalments
(box F28 less box F29. Copy this figure to box WS1 on form IHT200WS) **F30** £

G **Estate in the UK where tax may be paid by instalments**

Do you wish to pay the tax on these assets by instalments? *(Tick appropriate box)* | No | | Yes |

Interests in land owned by the deceased at the date of death

Open market value at the date of death

- Deceased's residence *(excluding farm houses)* — G1 £
- Other residential property — G2 £
- Farms, farmland, farm buildings and farmhouses. — G3 £
- Business property *(from which the deceased ran a business alone or in partnership)* — G4 £
- Timber and woodland which is not part of a farm. — G5 £
- Other land, buildings and rights over land — G6 £

	Interest in a business	Interest in a partnership	
- Farming business — G7.1 £ — G7.2 £ — G7 £

| | Interest in a business | Interest in a partnership | |
- Other business interests — G8.1 £ — G8.2 £ — G8 £

| | Farm trade assets | Other business assets | |
- Business assets — G9.1 £ — G9.2 £ — G9 £

- Quoted shares and securities, control holding only — G10 £

| | Control holding | Non-control holding | |
- Unquoted shares — G11.1 £ — G11.2 £ — G11 £

| | Control holding | Non-control holding | |
- Traded unquoted shares — G12.1 £ — G12.2 £ — G12 £

Total assets *(sum of boxes G1 to G12)* — G13 £

Liabilities, exemptions and reliefs *(that relate to the assets described in this section)*.

- Name and address of mortgagee

G14 £

- Other liabilities

Total of other liabilities — G15 £

Net total of assets less liabilities *(box G13 less boxes G14 and G15)* — G16 £

- Exemptions and reliefs

Total exemptions and reliefs — G17 £

Chargeable value of assets in the UK where tax may be paid by instalments *(box G16 less box G17)* — G18 £

H Summary of the chargeable estate

You should fill in form IHT200WS so that you can copy the figures to this section and to section J. If you are applying for a grant without the help of a solicitor or other agent and you do not wish to work out the tax yourself, leave this section and section J blank. Go on to section K. The corresponding box numbers from the IHT200WS are shown in *italics*.

Assets where tax may not be paid by instalments

- Estate in the UK *(box WS1)* H1 £
- Joint property - passing by survivorship *(box WS2)* H2 £
- Foreign property *(box WS3)* H3 £
- Settled property on which the trustees would like to pay tax now *(box WS4)* H4 £

    Total of assets where tax may not be paid by instalments *(box WS5)* H5 £

Assets where tax may be paid by instalments

- Estate in the UK *(box WS6)* H6 £
- Joint property - passing by survivorship *(box WS7)* H7 £
- Foreign property *(box WS8)* H8 £
- Settled property on which the trustees would like to pay tax now *(box WS9)* H9 £

    Total of assets where tax may be paid by instalments *(box WS10)* H10 £

Other property taken into account to calculate the total tax

- Settled property *(box WS11)* H11 £
- Alternatively secured pension *(box WS11A)* H11A £
- Gift with reservation *(box WS12)* H12 £

    Chargeable estate *(box WS13)* H13 £

    Cumulative total of lifetime transfers *(box WS14)* H14 £

    Aggregate chargeable transfer *(box WS15)* H15 £

J Calculating the tax liability

Calculating the total tax that is payable

- Aggregate chargeable transfer *(box WS16)* | J1 | £
- Tax threshold *(box WS17)* | J2 |
- Value chargeable to tax *(box WS18)* | J3 | £

Tax payable *(box WS19)* | J4 | £

- Tax (if any) payable on lifetime transfers *(box WS20)* | J5 | £
- Relief for successive charges *(box WS21)* | J6 | £

Tax payable on total of assets liable to tax *(box WS22)* | J7 | £

Calculating the tax payable on delivery of this account

- Tax which may not be paid by instalments *(box TX4)* | J8 | £
- Double taxation relief *(box TX5)* | J9 | £
- Interest to be added *(box TX7)* | J10 | £

Tax and interest being paid now which may not be paid by instalments *(box TX8)* | J11 | £

- Tax which may be paid by instalments *(box TX12)* | J12 | £
- Double taxation relief *(box TX13)* | J13 | £
- Number of instalments being paid now | J14 | / 10 | *(box TX15)*
- Tax now payable *(box TX16)* | J15 | £
- Interest on instalments to be added *(box TX17)* | J16 | £
- Additional interest to be added *(box TX18)* | J17 | £

Tax and interest being paid now which may be paid by instalments *(box TX19)* | J18 | £

Total tax and interest being paid now on this account *(box TX20)* | J19 | £

K Authority for repayment of inheritance tax

In the event of any inheritance tax being overpaid the payable order for overpaid tax and interest in connection with this estate should be made out to

Ⓛ Declaration

Note: you may be liable to a penalty if you deliver this account late. See the declaration below for other circumstances in which a penalty may be imposed.

I/We wish to apply for a [L1]

To the best of my/our knowledge and belief, the information I/we have given and the statements I/we have made in this account and in supplementary pages [L2]

attached (together called "this account") are correct and complete (list the supplementary pages used).

I/We have made the fullest enquiries that are reasonably practicable in the circumstances to find out the open market value of all the items shown in this account. The value of items in box(es) (list the boxes)

[L3]   are provisional

estimates which are based on all the information available to me/us at this time. I/We will tell Capital Taxes the exact value(s) as soon as I/we know it and I/we will pay any additional tax and interest that may be due.

I/We understand that I/we may be liable to prosecution if I/we deliberately conceal any information that affects the liability to inheritance tax arising on the deceased's death, OR if I/we deliberately include information in this account which I/we know to be false.

I/We understand that I/we may have to pay financial penalties if this account is incorrect by reason of my/our fraud or negligence, OR if I/we fail to remedy anything in this account which is incorrect in any material respect within a reasonable time of it coming to my/our notice.

I/We understand that the issue of the grant does not mean that

- I/we have paid all the inheritance tax and interest that may be due on the estate, or

- the statements made and the values included in this account are accepted by Capital Taxes.

I/We understand that Capital Taxes

- will only look at this account in detail after the grant has been issued

- may need to ask further questions and discuss the value of items shown in this account

- may make further calculations of tax and interest payable to help the persons liable for the tax make   provision to meet the tax liability.

I/We understand that where we have elected to pay tax by instalments that I/we may have to pay interest on any unpaid tax according to the law.

Each person delivering this account, whether as executor, intending administrator or otherwise must sign below to indicate that they have read and agreed the statements above.

Full name and address	Full name and address
Signature *Date*	*Signature* *Date*
Full name and address	Full name and address
Signature *Date*	*Signature* *Date*

Trust form 41G

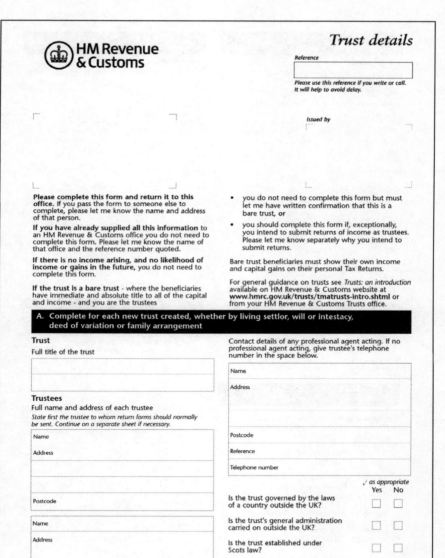

HM Revenue & Customs

Trust details

Reference

Please use this reference if you write or call. It will help to avoid delay.

Issued by

Please complete this form and return it to this office. If you pass the form to someone else to complete, please let me know the name and address of that person.

If you have already supplied all this information to an HM Revenue & Customs office you do not need to complete this form. Please let me know the name of that office and the reference number quoted.

If there is no income arising, and no likelihood of income or gains in the future, you do not need to complete this form.

If the trust is a bare trust - where the beneficiaries have immediate and absolute title to all of the capital and income - and you are the trustees

- you do not need to complete this form but must let me have written confirmation that this is a bare trust, or

- you should complete this form if, exceptionally, you intend to submit returns of income as trustees. Please let me know separately why you intend to submit returns.

Bare trust beneficiaries must show their own income and capital gains on their personal Tax Returns.

For general guidance on trusts see *Trusts: an introduction* available on HM Revenue & Customs website at **www.hmrc.gov.uk/trusts/tmatrusts-intro.shtml** or from your HM Revenue & Customs Trusts office.

A. Complete for each new trust created, whether by living settlor, will or intestacy, deed of variation or family arrangement

Trust
Full title of the trust

Trustees
Full name and address of each trustee
State first the trustee to whom return forms should normally be sent. Continue on a separate sheet if necessary.

Name

Address

Postcode

Name

Address

Postcode

Contact details of any professional agent acting. If no professional agent acting, give trustee's telephone number in the space below.

Name

Address

Postcode

Reference

Telephone number

	✓ as appropriate	
---	Yes	No
Is the trust governed by the laws of a country outside the UK?	☐	☐
Is the trust's general administration carried on outside the UK?	☐	☐
Is the trust established under Scots law?	☐	☐
Is the trust employment related?	☐	☐
Is this a trust for a vulnerable beneficiary? See *Trusts: an introduction.*	☐	☐

41G(Trust)

HMRC 03/06

B. Complete if trust established by will or intestacy

The deceased

Full name and last address of the deceased

Name

Address

Postcode

Date of death   /   /

Date trust commenced   /   /

HM Revenue & Customs office that dealt with the deceased's last Tax Return or received the probate, letters of administration, etc.

Reference in that office **or** National Insurance number

Administration period

        ✓ *as appropriate*
        Yes   No

Has the administration period ended? ☐ ☐

If yes, give the date it ended   /   /

C. Complete if trust established by deed of variation or family arrangement

Tick the relevant box only if the trust established by the deed of variation or family arrangement is

• additional to the will trust ☐
  if so, complete part B above and also give details at part A

• a replacement for the will trust ☐
  if so, do not complete part B above but give details at part A.

In either case, complete part D to give details of each person who took less under the deed than they would have done under the will - each person is a settlor of the amount given up.

D. Complete if trust established in settlor's lifetime

Date trust established (if under a deed of variation, etc., this is the date of the deed)   /   /

Settlor

Full name and address of settlor
Where there is more than one settlor you should give details for each, using a separate sheet if necessary.

Name

Address

Postcode

HM Revenue & Customs office that deals with the settlor's tax affairs

Reference in that office **or** National Insurance number

E. Complete for all trusts

Assets settled

Give details of the assets settled by each settlor, including values. Use a separate sheet if necessary. *If land or buildings, state the address. If shares, state number, class and Company Registration Number.*

Signature

Capacity in which signed

Full name in *CAPITALS*

Date   /   /

Data Protection Act

The normal Data Protection Act rules apply to this form. For more information log onto **www.hmrc.gov.uk/about/privacy.htm**

USEFUL ADDRESSES

Government

HM Revenue & Customs Inheritance Tax

More information and explanatory leaflets about IHT can be obtained from the HM Revenue & Customs Inheritance Tax offices.

HM Revenue & Customs Inheritance Tax (England and Wales)
Ferrers House
PO Box 38
Castle Meadow Road
Nottingham NG2 1BB
Helpline: 0845 302 0900 (probate and Inheritance Tax helpline)
Email: InheritanceTaxCustomerService@gtnet.gov.uk
www.hmrc.gov.uk

HM Revenue & Customs Inheritance Tax (Scotland)
Meldrum House
15 Drumsheugh Gardens
Edinburgh EH3 7UG
Tel: 0131 777 4050/4060
Helpline: 0845 302 0900 (probate and Inheritance Tax helpline)
Email: InheritanceTaxCustomerService@gtnet.gov.uk
www.hmrc.gov.uk

Companies House

The main functions of Companies House are to incorporate and dissolve limited companies, examine and store company information and make this information available to the public. The website contains useful information on setting up a limited company and all the relevant forms and guidance notes can be downloaded from the website.

Companies House
Crown Way
Maindy
Cardiff CF14 3UZ
Tel: 0870 33 33 636
Email: enquiries@companies-house.gov.uk
www.companieshouse.gov.uk

Communities and Local Government

Communities and Local Government is the department that deals with housing policy in the UK. If your child is a key worker and/or on a low income he may be able to receive financial help when he buys a house. There are various schemes available and more information about each scheme can be obtained from the website or by contacting the department at the address below.

Communities and Local Government
Eland House
Bressenden Place
London SW1E 5DU
Tel: 020 7944 4400
Email: contactus@communities.gov.uk
www.communities.gov.uk/housing

Inland Revenue Trusts

All UK resident trusts are dealt with by three Inland Revenue Trusts offices. Contact the office closest to where you live and it will be able to help with your enquiry.

Inland Revenue Trusts
Meldrum House
15 Drumsheugh Gardens
Edinburgh EH3 7UL
Tel: 0131 777 4343
Fax: 0131 777 4035

Inland Revenue Trusts
Lysnoweth
Infirmary Hill
Truro
Cornwall TR1 2JD
Tel: 01872 245 403
Fax: 01872 245 315

Inland Revenue Trusts
Huntingdon Court
90–94 Mansfield Road
Nottingham NG1 3HG
Tel: 0115 911 6500
Fax: 0115 911 6501/2

Trade and professional associations

The Association of Independent Inventory Clerks

The Association of Independent Inventory Clerks (AIIC) was set up in 1996 to represent inventory clerks and provide information to tenants and landlords. If you want to use an independent inventory clerk, you can find one in your area by using the online directory.

The Association of Independent Inventory Clerks
PO Box 1288
West End
Woking
Surrey GU24 9WE
Tel/fax: 01276 855 388
Email: centraloffice@aiic.uk.com
www.aiic.uk.com

The Residential Landlords Association

The Residential Landlords Association provides a range of products, services and advice to its members. There is a fee to pay if you decide to join, but once you become a member you are able to access information useful to you as a landlord.

The Residential Landlords Association
1 Roebuck Lane
Sale
Manchester M33 7SY
Tel: 0845 666 5000
Fax: 0845 665 1845
Email: info@rla.org.uk
www.rla.org.uk

The National Landlords Association

The National Landlords Association (NLA) provides a range of services to members and you may find it useful to join if you are hoping to remain as a landlord for some time.

National Landlords Association
22–26 Albert Embankment
London SE1 7TJ
Tel: 020 7840 8900
Fax: 0871 247 7535
Email: info@landlords.org.uk
www.landlords.org.uk

The British Bankers' Association

The British Bankers' Association (BBA) represents the banking industry in the UK. It is involved with the development and production of the Banking Code, produces a series of personal finance fact sheets for the general public, offers advice on money laundering and produces a variety of useful statistics and publications on finance in the UK.

British Bankers' Association
Pinners Hall
105–108 Old Broad Street
London EC2N 1EX
Tel: 020 7216 8800
Email: use contact form on website
www.bba.org.uk

The Council of Mortgage Lenders

The Council of Mortgage Lenders (CML) is the trade association for the mortgage lending industry in the UK. The organisation provides a range of general information for the consumer, including guides about home buying and selling, equity release products, buy-to-let products and mortgage information.

Council of Mortgage Lenders
Bush House
North West Wing
Aldwych
London WC2B 4PJ
Tel: 0845 373 6771
Email: info@cml.org.uk
www.cml.org.uk

The Society of Will Writers and Estate Planning Practitioners

The Society of Will Writers and Estate Planning Practitioners is a non-profit making, self-regulatory organisation which seeks to protect the public and serve the interests of its members. You can use the members' directory on the website to search for a Will Writer or estate planner in your area.

The Society of Will Writers
Eagle House
Exchange Road
Lincoln LN6 3JZ
Tel: 01522 68 78 88
Email: info@willwriters.com
www.thesocietyofwillwriters.co.uk

Institute of Professional Will Writers

The Institute of Professional Will Writers was founded in 1991 as a 'self-regulatory body to safeguard the public from unqualified practitioners and unethical business practices'. You can find a member in your area by using the online directory.

Institute of Professional Will Writers
Trinity Point
New Road
Halesowen
West Midlands B63 3HY
Tel: 08456 442 042
Fax: 08456 442 043
Email: office@ipw.org.uk
www.ipw.org.uk

Society of Trust and Estate Practitioners

The Society of Trust and Estate Practitioners (STEP) is a professional body that provides an international learning and business network for its members, who are professionals specialising in trusts and estates, executorship, administration and related taxes. You can find a practitioner in your area by contacting STEP.

Society of Trust and Estate Practitioners (STEP) Worldwide
26 Grosvenor Gardens
London SW1W 0GT
Tel: 020 7838 4890
Fax: 020 7838 4886
Email: step@step.org
www.step.org

National Association of Estate Agents

The National Association of Estate Agents (NAEA) was founded in 1962 and is a professional body for estate agency. The Federation of Overseas Property Developers, Agents and Consultants (FOPDAC) recently merged with the NAEA and you can find out more information about buying a property in the UK and overseas from this organisation.

National Association of Estate Agents
Arbon House
6 Tournament Court
Edgehill Drive
Warwick CV34 6LG
Tel: 01926 496 800
Fax: 01926 417 788
Email: info@naea.co.uk
www.naea.co.uk

The Ombudsman for Estate Agents

The Ombudsman for Estate Agents (OEA) has been established to provide a free, fair and independent service to buyers and sellers of residential property in the UK. You can search for an agent using the online directory.

Ombudsman for Estate Agents
Beckett House
4 Bridge Street
Salisbury
Wiltshire SP1 2LX
Tel: 01722 333 306
Fax: 01722 332 296
Email: admin@oea.co.uk
www.oea.co.uk

The Federation of Master Builders

The Federation of Master Builders (FMB) is a trade association representing small- and medium-sized businesses in the UK. You can find a member by using the online directory.

The Federation of Master Builders
Gordon Fisher House
14–15 Great James Street
London WC1N 3DP
Tel: 020 7242 7583
Fax: 020 7404 0296
Email: central@fmb.org.uk
www.fmb.org.uk

Information and advice services

Energy Saving Trust

The Energy Saving Trust was established by the UK government to address the issue of climate change. The organisation provides free and impartial advice to members of the public who are interested in saving energy. There is also a network of local advice centres (contact details available on the website) and a national helpline for free, independent and local energy saving advice (0800 512 012).

Energy Saving Trust – England
21 Dartmouth Street
London SW1H 9BP
Tel: 020 7222 0101
Email: use feedback form on website
www.energysavingtrust.org.uk

Energy Saving Trust – Scotland
112/2 Commercial Street
Leith
Edinburgh EH6 6NF
Tel: 0131 555 7900

Energy Saving Trust – Wales
2 Caspian Way
Cardiff Bay
Cardiff CF10 4DQ
Tel: 029 2046 8340

Energy Saving Trust – Northern Ireland
Enterprise House
55/59 Adelaide Street
Belfast BT2 8FE
Tel: 028 9072 6006

Charities

The Empty Homes Agency

The Empty Homes Agency is an independent, campaigning charity, which exists to highlight the waste of empty property in England and Wales. On the website you can find useful information on buying, owning and renovating an empty property, including information about local authority grants and energy efficiency grants. It also contains links to organisations that are willing to provide mortgages on empty properties.

Empty Homes Agency
1 London Bridge
London SE1 9BG
Tel: 020 7022 1870
Email: info@emptyhomes.com
www.emptyhomes.com

The Electrical Safety Council

The Electrical Safety Council is an independent charity committed to reducing deaths and injuries through electrical accidents at home and at work. You can find more information about electrical safety on the website and use the online directory to find a registered electrician in your area.

Electrical Safety Council
18 Buckingham Gate
London SW1E 6LB
Tel: 0870 040 0561
Fax: 0870 040 0560
Email: enquiries@electricalsafetycouncil.org.uk
www.electricalsafetycouncil.org.uk

Union

The National Union of Students

More information about all aspects of student housing can be obtained from the National Union of Students (NUS).

National Union of Students
2nd floor, Centro 3
Mandela Street
London NW1 0DU
Tel: 0871 221 8221
Fax: 0871 221 8222
Email: nusuk@nus.org.uk
www.nusonline.com

Insurance

Guarantee Protection Insurance

Guarantee Protection Insurance (GPI) was authorised by the FSA to trade and issue insurance certificates in the UK in April 2002. You can find out more information about this type of insurance from the address below.

Guarantee Protection Insurance
8 Alloway Place
Ayr
South Ayrshire KA7 2AA
Tel: 01292 268 020
Fax: 01292 611 723
Email: info@gptprotection.co.uk
www.gptprotection.co.uk

USEFUL WEBSITES

Government

www.landregistry.gov.uk

On this site you can find out about average house prices throughout England and Wales, narrowing your search to specific postcode areas. If you are interested in finding out more about a specific property, there is a small fee for the service.

www.ros.gov.uk

This is the website of the Registers of Scotland Executive Agency. This is a government agency that is responsible for compiling and maintaining registers relating to property and other legal documents. On this website you can obtain information about house prices in Scotland. There is a small fee for obtaining details about specific properties.

www.fsa.gov.uk

This is the website of the FSA, the UK's financial watchdog. On the website you can find a wide range of financial information, including advice and guidance about buying a home, choosing a mortgage, arranging a pension and seeking financial advice. Some useful tools on the website include a budget calculator, debt test and pension calculator. You can also access the register of regulated firms and their agents and find out about unregulated firms that are targeting UK households on this website.

www.hmcourts-service.gov.uk

You can obtain information about probate registries from HMCS. On their website you can use the search facility to find a registry in your area. All registries are open Monday to Friday. Most are open 9.30am to 4pm, although there may be some local variations in times.

www.hmrc.gov.uk

The HM Revenue & Customs website provides a range of useful information for individuals and employees, employers and businesses and corporations. On this website you can also find guidelines and application forms for people applying for a 'grant of representation' (England, Wales and Northern Ireland) or a 'grant of confirmation' (Scotland), along with useful information about taxes and trusts.

www.scotcourts.gov.uk

The Scottish Court Service (SCS) is an Executive Agency which is responsible for the administration of the Supreme and Sheriff Courts in Scotland. On the website you can obtain contact details and opening times of court buildings and public counters.

www.direct.gov.uk

This is the government information website that brings together public service advice, guidance and information. On this site you can access information about paying Inheritance Tax and taking advantage of various exemptions and reliefs.

www.businesslink.gov.uk

This is the government website that provides practical advice and guidance for people hoping to set up a business and for those already in business. On the website you can access useful information about producing profit/loss plans and cash flow forecasts. You can also enter your postcode to receive advice and information from your local Business Link centre.

Finance, banking and insurance

www.hbosplc.com

The Halifax UK House Price Index was launched in 1984. On the website you can find useful historical data about the movement of the housing market, based on mortgage lending. It is possible to access a map of the UK and click on a particular region to find out the average house price, the quarterly change and annual change, compared to the national average.

www.nationwide.co.uk

On this website you can access the Nationwide House Price Index and other useful housing information. It is possible to find out how the value of a property has changed over the years by entering the postcode into the House Price Calculator available on the website. There is also a variety of reports about trends and prospects in the housing market that will be useful for your background research.

www.scottishwidows.co.uk

This is the Scottish Widows website where you can find more information about the Scottish Widows IHT Index. There is also a useful IHT Calculator available that will calculate any potential IHT which may be due.

www.directline.com

This is the website of Direct Line, which provides various types of insurance. On the website you can access information about the Direct Line UK Second Property Index.

www.confused.com
www.moneysupermarket.com
www.comparethemarket.com
www.insurancewide.com

These are four well-known and reputable insurance comparison sites and they will provide a useful starting point for your research into the best insurance deals on the market.

Housing

www.nalscheme.co.uk

The National Approved Letting Scheme (NALS) is an accreditation scheme for lettings and management agents. Members agree to meet defined standards of customer service and must have in place the necessary insurances to protect clients' money. You can find a member in your area by using the online directory.

www.thedisputeservice.co.uk
www.depositprotection.com
www.mydeposits.co.uk

These are the websites of the three companies that have been awarded the contract to administer tenancy deposit schemes. More information about each of these schemes can be obtained from these websites.

www.housing.nhs.uk

This is the Housing for NHS Staff website. If your child works for the NHS he can find more information about the schemes that are available to help him to buy a home. It may be prudent for your child to take advantage of these schemes rather than receive financial help from his parents, although he should seek specialist advice first.

www.home.co.uk

On this website you can access information about house prices in all parts of the United Kingdom since April 2000. You can also use the postcode calculator to find out house prices within your postcode. The service is free and provides a wide range of useful housing information for buyers, sellers and investors.

Utilities

www.niceic.com

NICEIC acts as the electrical contracting industry's independent voluntary regulatory body for electrical installation safety matters throughout the UK. You can find out more about electrical safety and obtain contact details of an approved contractor in your area from this website.

www.trustcorgi.com

CORGI is considered to be the leading authority for information on gas safety issues around the home. You can find more information about gas safety, rules and regulations on this website and you can use the online directory to find a qualified installer in your area.

Trade and professional associations

www.thepfs.org

The Personal Finance Society (PFS) is the largest professional body for individual financial advisers and those in related roles in the UK. You can use its online service to find a financial adviser in your area and access useful information on getting the most out of your adviser and knowing how to choose the right person.

www.lawsociety.org.uk

This is the website of the Law Society. Through the 'solicitors online' facility you can search the database by firm name, postcode or location, country or area of law to find a suitable solicitor for your needs.

www.napit.org.uk

This is the website of the National Association of Professional Inspectors and Testers. All NAPIT members carrying out domestic work in the UK are part of the Government Trustmark scheme, which signifies that a business has insurance, good health and safety practices and good customer care. Also, all NAPIT members are backed by a full six-year guarantee for the workmanship. You can find a member by using the online database.

Information and advice services

www.clsdirect.org.uk

The Community Legal Service has been set up to provide members of the public with legal information and advice. On the website you can access a series of free information leaflets about Wills, inheritance, separation and divorce. There is also a useful 'advice search' section that enables you to search for legal advice by topic.

www.litrg.org.uk

This is the website of the Low Incomes Tax Reform Group, which is an initiative that has been set up by the Chartered Institute of Taxation to provide advice and information for people on low incomes. If your child is on a low income he should be encouraged to visit this website as he may be able to reduce his tax bill and find out whether he is eligible to receive tax credits.

www.citizensadvice.org.uk

This is the Citizens Advice Bureau website. You can obtain details of your local CAB by using the online directory.

www.adviceguide.org.uk

This is the information, advice and guidance website of the Citizens Advice Bureau. On this site you can find useful information on many topics, including property, investment, legal issues and finance.

Research and consultancy

www.savills.co.uk

This is a company that offers a consultancy service and conducts research into the property market in the UK and Europe. On its website you can find information about its research into the second-home property market.

Further reading

Ahuja, A. (2008) *The Buy-to-Let Bible*, 4th edition, London: Lawpack Publishing Ltd.

Bayley, C. (2006) *How to Avoid Inheritance Tax*, 2nd edition, Kirkcaldy: Taxcafe UK Limited.

Bayley, C. (2006) *Using a Property Company to Save Tax*, 2nd edition, Kirkcaldy: Taxcafe UK Limited.

Bradshaw, J. (2007) *House Buying, Selling and Conveyancing*, 5th edition, London: Lawpack Publishing Ltd.

Davies, J. (2006) *Buying Property Abroad*, 2nd edition, London: Which? Books.

Dawson, C. (2007) *The Complete Guide to Buying, Selling and Investing in Green Property*, London: Kogan Page.

Dawson, C. (2007) *The Complete Guide to Property Development for Small Investors*, 2nd edition, London: Kogan Page.

Farrell, D. (2006) *The Jet-to-Let Bible: The Secrets of Overseas Property Investment*, London: Lawpack Publishing Ltd.

Gooddie, H. (2007) *Buying Bargains at Property Auctions*, 4th edition, London: Lawpack Publishing Ltd.

Hodgkinson, L. (2007) *The Complete Guide to Buying Property Abroad*, 6th edition, London: Kogan Page.

Knight, J. (2005) *Wills, Probate & Inheritance Tax for Dummies*, Chichester: John Wiley and Sons Ltd.

Lowe, J. (2005) *The Which? Guide to Giving and Inheriting: Tax Efficient Ways to Pass on Money, Property and Other Valuables*, 8th edition, London: Which? Books.

Scott, M. (2007) *The 'Daily Telegraph' How to Avoid the Inheritance Tax Trap*, London: Constable and Robinson.

Tomlinson, L. (2008) *How to Make Money from Student Property*, London: Lawpack Publishing Ltd.

Williams, H. (2007) *How to Save Inheritance Tax*, London: Lawpack Publishing Ltd.

Index